Managing the Pressures
in Teaching

Managing the Pressures in Teaching:
Practical Ideas for Tutors and Their Students

Stephen Cox and Ruth Heames

FALMER PRESS

Taylor & Francis Group

UK	Falmer Press, 1 Gunpowder Square, London, EC4A 3DE
USA	Falmer Press, Taylor & Francis Inc., 325 Chestnut Street, 8th Floor, Philadelphia, PA 19106

First published in 1999

A catalogue record for this book is available from the British Library

ISBN 0 7507 0836 0 cased
ISBN 0 7507 0835 2 paper

Library of Congress Cataloging-in-Publication Data are available on request

Jacket design by Caroline Archer

Typeset in 11/13 Garamond by
Graphicraft Limited, Hong Kong

Printed in Great Britain by Biddles Ltd., Guildford and King's Lynn on paper which has a specified pH value on final paper manufacture of not less than 7.5 and is therefore 'acid free'.

Every effort has been made to contact copyright holders for their permission to reprint material in this book. The publishers would be grateful to hear from any copyright holder who is not here acknowledged and will undertake to rectify any errors or omissions in future editions of this book.

Contents

Contents

List of Photocopiable Proformas

List of Photocopiable Proformas

Acknowledgment

The authors wish to thank Sue and Trevor Habeshaw for their help and encouragement during the early stages of preparing this work.

Chapter 1

Introduction: Managing the Pressures in Teaching

When I am hassled about something, I always stop and ask myself what difference it will make in the evolution of the human species in the next million years, and that question always helps me to get back my perspective. Anne Wilson Schaef (1990)

Introduction

The climate in education has changed and will continue to change. A major factor has been the increase in direction and control from central government, not least in the imposition of so called 'efficiency gains' — cuts. This has created an environment in which tutors have to react to demands and circumstances under seemingly ever-increasing pressure.

This book is written to encourage you to take time out from that 'I'm too busy' syndrome and consider your role as a tutor and how you manage that role on a daily basis. It has been designed to offer you practical ideas for reducing the pressures for both yourself and your students within the teaching and learning experience.

In this context the story of Handy's (1990) frog is an illuminating allegory for our times.

A small frog lived in a shallow pond in a tropical area at a time of rapid climatic change. He found that he could adjust to the warming climate by making a series of small adjustments to his lifestyle that enabled him to cope without too much personal discomfort. For instance, as the water in his pond became progressively warmer, he found he had to spend more time on his lily-pad, with the result that he began to suffer from progressive deterioration of his skin. His diet also changed, because with the warming climate, the insect life over his pond changed. This meant that there were fewer and fewer of his favourite insects for him to eat, and he began to get more and more digestive problems. However, by making these and other similar small but constant changes to his lifestyle, he managed to survive, although in gradually escalating discomfort. Occasionally, he had vague, disquieting half memories of a happier time gone by, when life seemed to be more comfortable and enjoyable, but as he was forced to concentrate more on thinking about when was the right time to enter the water because it was getting too hot or wondering if a new insect would be good to eat, he had less and less time to think about the past and what life had been like. This process went on for a considerable time, and there was a continual decline in his living conditions and the frog's life became less and less enjoyable, and more and more of a strain — until one fatal day, he leapt from his lily-pad into the pond, and died almost instantly — because the water was boiling.

Many tutors find themselves in a position analogous to that of the frog. Through a continual series of small adjustments over the years in response to pressures in their environment, they find themselves in a new and, in some cases, potentially life threatening situation. To pursue the frog analogy one stage further, one restorative strategy might be to migrate to a new and deeper pond further north (or south) where conditions are once more life-enhancing. This does not mean that we have to cease being (frogs) tutors, but that instead we adopt carefully thought-out strategies and practices that are compatible with our new and considerably changed surroundings.

The impact of these changes is also felt by students.

> Students have also been placed under increasing stress. The transition for post-secondary school students from small, tightly-knit, closely-supervised groups studying three or four subjects, to different large groups of one hundred or more in each of up to eight modules can be very traumatic. They now have greater financial problems than ever before, and are taught in larger groups, often working on their own or with their peers for long periods. . . . (Cox and Heames, 1997)

There is a lot at stake: quality assessment, league tables, contracts all add to the pressure that tutors and students are under.

Tutors have always had a multi-dimensional role, including those of assessor, tutor, counsellor, researcher, administrator, manager, consultant, scholar and curriculum developer. These, combined with the additional external pressures, mean that role conflict, overload and role stress are now becoming commonplace.

Financial exigencies have forced institutions to appoint more tutors on part-time, short contracts. They now tend to have less support from their institutions than in the past, and they often miss out on staff development programmes, information and other activities.

With the background of constant change in mind, this book provides you with practical ideas that you can use to make your teaching (and learning) a more manageable and pleasurable experience for you and your students. It will enable you to become more strategic, and therefore more adaptable to future change.

How to Use this Book

This book is written to provide ideas and activities to be dipped into as the need arises. Of course, you are welcome to read it from cover to cover if you wish, but afterwards we hope you will return to it from time to time to apply it in your teaching. Please feel free to modify and adapt the ideas and to build upon them in your teaching in the way that suits you. It is not intended to be an inclusive guide to every aspect of teaching. What it does do is to address some of the main issues in organizing teaching and learning experiences and in developing a supportive environment in which students can learn effectively. At the end of most chapters we have included photocopiable proformas of further activities for your use.

The tutor's main role is to organize and facilitate students' learning experiences. This book is based on the premise that learning is a partnership between students and tutors, and that the students, if provided with the right support and milieu, can make valuable contributions from their previous knowledge, their reflections and sharing them with their peers and tutors. It is assumed that learning is an active process that involves reflection as a fundamental component. Burge (1989) suggests that when devising and operating courses, tutors might consider:

- promoting reflective learning and asking students to think 'What have I learned?' and 'Why is it significant for me?';
- using learning contracts as far as possible;
- giving real choices for learners regarding sequence, pacing, content process and assessments of learning;
- supporting risk-taking by learners;
- using project work, analysis of real life situations, theory building and experiential techniques;
- promoting learning partnerships as far as possible.

Taking this approach a stage forward, the book is designed to enable you to engage in its contents and use this as an active learning

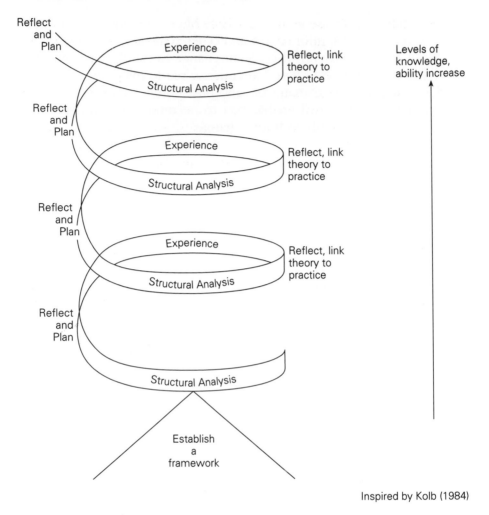

Inspired by Kolb (1984)

Figure 1.1   Active Learning: A developmental model

opportunity yourself. It is for you to identify those components that will help you most and then to take the following steps:

- select the idea(s) from the book that meet(s) your immediate teaching needs;
- assimilate the suggestions;
- reflect on their value in the context of your own teaching;
- plan how to incorporate these ideas into the learning experience for your students;
- implement the plan;
- ask the students to evaluate the session;

- reflect on the session as a whole by
    - describing the session as it happened, identifying critical events
    - recording your feelings at particular points
    - noting thoughts surrounding the session and any critical aspects that occurred
    - examining your reactions to the processes and activities in the session (for instance, did you interrupt discussion at an inappropriate point?)
- evaluate the total experience, not forgetting the students' feedback as well as your own, bringing together an informed judgment on the value of the session for you and your students.

This description of the learning process has been stimulated by the work of Kolb (1984), see Figure 1.1. As shown in the diagram, the cycle is three dimensional since it resembles a spiral in which with each iteration the quality of the learning experience is improved. Furthermore, previous knowledge and practical experience inform the acquisition of new knowledge.

Chapter 2

Helping Students to Reduce their Levels of Stress in the Classroom

Entering higher or further education for the first time is a major life changing event. For some students, the transition is smooth and just another stage in their development. For others, it is a very stressful time with many adjustments to be made.

The first session is an important one; first impressions do count. It is essential that members of the group become familiar with one another and are comfortable working together, as well as learning about the programme of studies and the tasks to be undertaken. If the group is to work together effectively, then the forming of the group is a necessary process. Establishing a sound communication system and group identity should be a priority and 'getting to know you' time is invaluable and indispensable, whether the group is formed for a semester, an academic year, or for the life of the course itself. Much learning emerges through the process of communication. If the tutor and the students are not comfortable with the classroom situation and its climate, then their ability to communicate, and therefore to learn, will be impaired.

This chapter identifies a number of activities and strategies that will help students to settle into their new courses or modules of study. They are designed to:

- foster good working relationships;
- identify the expectations and demands of the programme;
- develop a framework for studying;
- help the students to achieve a sense of direction.

Introductions

Ice breaking techniques can be simple ways to remove barriers and enable students to get to know one another and the tutor. They can also begin the important process of building a positive working relationship.

There are many introductory activities that help students to get to know one another. This example is effective and straightforward to operate. Proforma 2.1 is included on p. 23.

How to run the activity: Introductions

1 Setting the scene
   Say to the class:
   The content of the discussion will remain within the group. You are encouraged to talk openly about yourselves but there is no compulsion to do so. Therefore, it is important to respect each others' information.

2 Working in pairs
   Divide the group into working pairs, then say:
   Each of you will interview your partner in turn for five minutes. I will tell you when time is up.
   (If there is an odd number in the class then form a group of three, or take your place as one of a pair.)
   Tell the students when to start, when to change roles and when to finish.

3 Screening
   At the end of the interview phase, say:
   Will each member of the pair please check out with your partner if they disclosed any information during the interview which they do not wish other members of the group to know at this stage.

4 Feedback (for groups of 16 maximum)
   Say to the class:
   Will each member of each pair please introduce his or her partner to the whole group, taking about two minutes each to do so.

5 Feedback (for groups of over 16)
   Progress by 'snowballing':
   Say:
   Will two pairs please join together to form a quartet and will each member of the group please introduce his or her partner in turn, taking about two minutes each.
   (Time allocated for this phase, 10 minutes)

Say:
*Please will you 'snowball' again, forming octets. Will those in
each octet then compile a list of the hobbies and interests that
members have and elect a spokesperson.*
(Time allocated 15 minutes)

Then say:
*Will the elected spokespersons please introduce members of their
octet to the whole group, and inform the whole group of the
octet's interests.*
(Time allocated n groups × 5 minutes)

Building Teams

Adjusting from being a pupil or worker to being a student can be
very stressful. It can be easy for new students to misunderstand what
role is expected of them. Working and communicating within larger
groups can also be very daunting. For example, many new students
come from classes of fifteen or fewer in school or college and very
rapidly they have to adjust to being a member of a cohort of 80, 100
or even 500.

For the tutor, managing the learning environment involves much
thought and planning about helping individuals to come together as a
cohesive group or set of groups. Group dynamics are very influential in
the progress and achievements of the group.

Frequently, student groups are asked to subdivide into smaller
units to progress a task, for example to brainstorm ideas, to form buzz
groups, or to carry out a practical exercise. Initially this can be threatening for students. It is all too easy for a more dominant member of the
group to assume the role of leader or become the 'expert' and mono-
polize the whole activity.

A team building exercise can be a very useful mechanism through
which to prepare the less confident and assertive students to develop
skills of participation and acceptance of new roles and responsibilities.
Equally, it is a means through which the more dominant students can
experience different roles than those they normally assume or are
assigned in groups. Such an activity assists the total communication
process, making the group situation feel more comfortable and less
stressed. Burton and Dimbleby (1995) state that 'The quality of verbal
and non-verbal interactions will determine the strength of the group'.

There are many ideas for developing teams to be found in management training and life skills manuals. The activity described here is enjoyable and effective for students. Proformas 2.2 and 2.3 for the game and the debriefing phase are included on pp. 24 and 25.

How to run the activity: Building Teams

CREATE A GAME

1   Equipment
    Ensure that the following equipment is available to each team:
    a watch
    pens and large sheets of paper, e.g. flip chart paper
    scissors, string and glue

2   Setting the scene
    Set the scene by discussing the aims of the session. Say to the class:
    This activity will enable you to get to know one another; give you the opportunity to practise working in groups; give you the opportunity to experience and reflect on group processes.
    Divide the class into teams of five or six, ideally, but this will depend on the working space available, and the size of the class. Give out the proformas.

3   Game design
    Teams must appoint a team leader and then undertake the task.

4   Feedback
        Reassemble the class.
        Call for volunteers to form groups to demonstrate each of the games created.
        Each team leader in turn selects and instructs a volunteer group how to play the game.
        Observers or other group members keep time and indicate when time is up.
        Each game is played in turn.
        The tutor calls the team leaders together and instructs them each to carry out an evaluation with the participants of their game.

Each team leader concurrently brings together the volunteers who played the game that the team leader's team devised and conducts an evaluation of the game.

5 Debriefing phase
Open a discussion on the processes which occurred throughout the activity. Include the following as triggers to encourage the discussion:

How did team members set about the task?
Did they set initial ground rules?
What roles emerged?
Were these roles necessary in order to complete the task?
How were the roles assigned/assumed?
How were decisions made?
Was the activity achieved in the given time?
How did members feel about being part of a group?
What advantages are there in using team work for a task?
(The tutor might wish to write these on a flip chart for use in later sessions)
How did the volunteers feel about the game?

Open the discussion for any other comments.

Close the activity by thanking the members for their participation. Sum up the key points from the activity itself and relate these to the aims set at the beginning of the session.

Clarifying Students' Roles

Making the transition into higher or further education is difficult for many students. Adjusting to the change in scale and culture between school and university or college can be very difficult. In particular, it can be problematic and stressful for students to behave as adult learners, and accept responsibility for their own learning. For instance, much of the work in higher and further education can be discussion, problem solving or group based rather than directed or controlled.

As tutors, we need to address explicitly the nature and expectations of the student role. It is important that students are fully aware of, and prepared for, the degree of independence that they are given, and the nature of the teamwork and cooperation that is expected of them in order to fulfil the learning objectives or outcomes. Without this awareness, students can become tense and anxious and they can miss their opportunities.

How to run the activity: Clarifying Students' Roles

To emphasize these roles for students, we might both say at induction or at the start of each module and write in the course guide or student handbook:

> *The module(s) is/are organized to allow you to make the most of the opportunities provided for you to make a contribution to the group, by expressing your ideas and opinions and sharing your experiences. As you progress towards your degree (or award) we expect you to assume increasing responsibility for your work. What is more, increasing amounts of this work will be undertaken out-side tutor/student contact time. My role as tutor is to:*
> * *bring together the programme of learning;*
> * *share my expertise with you;*
> * *facilitate group and individual learning; and*
> * *organize the resources to provide the support to help you to learn effectively and efficiently.*

It is essential to repeat this, especially in the early stages of the course or module, and make sure also that students have the same message in print — perhaps in the Student Handbook. You could also use the photocopiable Proforma 2.4 on p. 26.

Setting Ground Rules

Classes of all kinds, but especially small groups such as tutorials and seminars can be stressful, unproductive or even severely disrupted when students do not appreciate that there are codes of behaviour that apply to these sessions. It is important that these ground rules are brought out into the open, discussed and agreed upon. It is normal to introduce the concept at the beginning of the course or module, but it is essential to return to it at intervals. In particular, it should be one of the first steps to raise the matter of ground rules again with a class if things are not going well.

One problem is that tutors assume that students know the ground rules. Often this is not the case, and students' stress and anxiety levels are raised because they do not understand the norms, roles and tasks that are expected of them. As a tutor, it is part of your role to manage the learning environment and therefore your responsibility to guide the students towards an agreed set of ground rules for the conduct of future classes.

How to run the activity: Setting Ground Rules

This exercise is written in the form of a script for the tutor, and can be used in conjunction with the Proforma 2.5 on p. 27.

1 *So that we can work together effectively as a group, it is import-ant that we identify both our expectations from the course/ module and the basis on which we are going to work. This is the way we are going to do it:*
On your own write down the answers to these questions. (They could be displayed on an overhead projector or a flip chart).
   - *Why are you here?*
   - *What do you hope to achieve by attending these sessions?*
   - *What do you think your role in class should be?*
   - *What is acceptable behaviour of other members of the class in terms of participation and attendance?*
   - *What can you expect of the tutor?*
   - *What would be the best way to handle sabotage?*
You have five minutes for this task.

2 *In pairs, share your ideas and discuss the similarities and differences between them. You have five minutes for this task.*

3 *In fours:*
   - *appoint a scribe and agree a common list of ground rules for the future conduct of this class*
   - *write them on an acetate sheet for the overhead pro-jector (or a sheet of flip chart paper).*
You have 10 minutes for this task.

4 *Now I'd like each group to report back. We will then select the common elements from the list and adopt these as the ground rules for the class.*

Alternative Activity

A livelier, but perhaps much riskier approach is to conduct a negative brainstorm. It is risky because it gives students bent upon being disrupt-ive a list of behaviours they can exploit. **This activity, therefore, is not recommended for groups that you do not know well, or that are negative or that contain a disruptive element.**

How to run the activity: Negative Brainstorm

1   Say to the class:
    We are are going to find out what behaviour and attitudes would be necessary to totally destroy any class. Call out your ideas, and I will list them on the board/overhead projector.
    List all the ideas as they come in.

2   Then say:
    How many of these do we see in our class?
    Tick off each one as it is identified.

3   Then say:
    Well, I don't know about you, but I am pretty upset to think that my class has been/could be operating on this set of rules. I am sure that you would like your classes to be fun and productive. Let's list instead the factors that would make our classes into the sort of experience we would like.

4   Put up a heading 'Ground rules for future classes' and ask for contributions from the class. Before you write each one up, first ask the class for comments and then either ask for a vote, or say:
    This is a new ground rule. Are we all agreed?

It is worth having a copy of the ground rules typed and distributed to all members of the class. Alternatively the list can be put on the wall each time the class meets. It is essential to revisit ground rules at intervals during the year, just to make sure that they are fresh in students' minds. You, as a tutor, can also use them to avert uncooperative or antisocial behaviour.

Developing Reflective Students

It has been acknowledged previously in this book that students are now often under considerable pressure. It is not solely pressure of adjustment, it can be sustained financial or academic pressure throughout the course. One approach to managing this is to identify exactly what is causing the feelings of pressure and stress. According to Cooper, Cooper and Eaker (1988):

any success in dealing with life stress must begin with self knowledge. If personal sources of stress can be identified then consideration can be given to strategies and practices that may minimise or eliminate these feelings of discomfort.

Essential to this process is developing the skill of reflection. This involves an in-depth review of events and experiences, followed by a critical appraisal that leads to the consideration of alternative strategies. Thus, reflection can help students to manage stressful situations more effectively by helping them to change. These changes can be in their behaviour, their learning or their self-management techniques.

By providing the framework and the opportunity to enable them to develop skills of reflection you are empowering students by giving them the responsibility for learning and promoting personal and academic independence. However, the mere instruction to '*Stop and reflect*' is a tall order. The question that automatically arises is '*How?*' The process of reflection is more than a moment's pondering on the event or experience. The technique of reflection needs to be discussed explicitly and students need to work through the process with guidance if it is to be thorough and beneficial. The process of reflection enables the individual to recall their own and others' behaviour, the feelings they experienced and the attitudes that were conveyed. Thus, the student is able to revisit an event or experience and analyse it to view it from a variety of perspectives and depths. What does the process involve? It can be taken at differing levels, very much in the way that a hierarchy of knowledge is built.

How to run the activity: Developing Reflective Students

Use this activity with photocopiable Proforma 2.6 on p. 28.

1   Say to the students:
    Think of a stressful event or experience connected with your recent academic work. Recall what happened in as much detail as you can.

    Share this with a partner. Help one another to identify key issues and critical incidents by asking questions to encourage your partner to explore and expand their recall. You might do this best by focusing on contributory factors, and asking questions such as 'What happened next?' and 'What was the result?'

    Explore the underlying factors by asking questions about the feelings, attitudes and actions that were part of the event.

Acknowledge the underlying principles and relate the theory to the actual event or experience. For instance, can you identify accepted principles or received wisdom that sheds positive light on what happened, such as the theory on defence mechanisms, group dynamics, physiological symptoms of stress?

2 Strategies for the future:
   Describe how you would like to deal with a similar situation if you are confronted with one in the future. Are there any strategies that would help you to build up your personal resources to help you cope better in future?

3 Debriefing:
   Debriefing to review what has been learnt and share the new knowledge.

From the detail above you can see that the art of reflection is in the systematic review of events and experiences to assist in the learning process. It enables us to be more prepared for the future. To reflect is not merely to commit a moment's thought.

Setting the Learning Agenda

It can be overwhelming and demotivating for students if tutors present the validated course document to students without making it user-friendly. (A version of it might be found in some Student Handbooks). It can be equally stressful for students to receive no information at all about what is to come and how it is to be studied.

Traditionally, it is the tutor who translates the aims and objectives or aims and learning outcomes into a scheme of work for the programme of study. A learning agenda is much more that a scheme of work. Its purpose is to:

- make sense of the learning objectives for students;
- share the vision of the learning experience;
- detail how tutor contact time will be spent;
- detail the topics to be covered — how and when;
- describe the expectations for students' independent study;
- clarify the preparation, such as pre-reading, required for each class.

The key factor for the tutor is both to challenge and support the students (that is to be a facilitator, or manager, of their learning) rather than being totally directive and a 'giver' of knowledge. It is all too easy in the early stages for the students to develop a passive role in the learning process.

How to Introduce the Learning Agenda

In introducing the learning agenda to students you might say:

> *Here is the learning agenda for the next few weeks. You will notice that this includes your learning objectives, as well as a description of what learning activities you can expect to be doing at what times and under what subject headings in order to achieve them.*

You might go on to explain the rationale for this — the reasons why you have chosen particular activities to help students master particular objectives in particular subject areas, and why the sequencing you have chosen is important.

> *As you progress into the second or third year/level of your programme, the emphasis will move towards you setting your own priority areas of the learning agenda under my guidance. By this stage, you should be acquiring the capacity to reflect and will be becoming capable of identifying your own strengths and weaknesses. At level three, it is feasible that the entire learning agenda will be student-led. At this level you will have grasped the fundamental concepts of the subject area and will be becoming familiar with handling the knowledge base in an evaluative way. By that time you will be experienced in judging your own needs for a fuller command of the subject.*

Creating a Positive Climate for Learning

An apparent lack of purpose and direction in the classroom can create tension, stress and anxiety. Generating a positive climate is essential for a productive and enjoyable learning experience. Otherwise, students can easily lose interest, motivation and commitment if the group experience and the climate do not feel comfortable. The teaching and learning experience is a partnership and so there are responsibilities from both tutors and students alike.

How to Generate a Positive Climate

As a tutor you can encourage the students to be:

- prepared to make a contribution and to share information and expertise;
- aware of the needs of other group members and non-judgmental about them;
- attentive, cooperative and prepared to accept responsibilities within the group;
- problem-solvers rather than 'sponges': this helps motivation;
- open, without hidden agendas;
- clear about and comfortable within their role as active learners.

To do this you should;

- make the learning agenda explicit and ensure that it is agreed by the class;
- explore the ground rules and ensure that all members of the group, including yourself, have a commitment to them;
- check that the students understand the teaching and learning process to be used and that their expectations about their roles and responsibilities are clarified and agreed;
- select appropriate learning tasks and methods;
- be fair in managing the group;
- be positive and open;
- be calm and rational when the unexpected occurs;
- establish a balance between seriousness and fun in learning;
- create space for thought and reflection;
- lead by modelling appropriate behaviour in conducting the class and the learning;
- be confident in your own ability to teach the material and knowledge of the subject;
- be creative in grouping the class for activities bearing in mind the notion of quality not quantity.

You can also organize the environment in which the class will work so that it is:

- appropriate for the nature of the session;
- a comfortable temperature with good ventilation;
- in a setting conducive to the learning method and task (including seating arrangements);

- possible for you to reach all members of the group to reduce communication and environmental barriers.

Hopson and Scally (1981) list further similar factors in an excellent table on pp. 163–7 of their book *Lifeskills Teaching*.

Developing Students' Awareness of their own Learning Methods and Styles

Students can enter higher or further education with very fixed and conservative ideas about what constitutes learning. Often this will be variations on the theme of memorizing information or repackaging facts for later regurgitation in lectures. This surface approach to learning does characterize some of the learning that many students have to do. It can prove very stressful for them, too, because it often involves them in ultimately vain attempts to learn by rote rather than through understanding.

One approach can be to make it very explicit for our students what sort of approaches to learning will be expected of them on the course or module that they are following. It can be helpful for them to distinguish between deep and surface learning, for instance.

How to run the activity: Developing Students' Awareness
of their Own Learning Methods and Styles

This exercise can be run in conjunction with the photocopiable Proforma 2.7 on p. 29.

1 Explain to the students some of the concepts of deep and surface learning. You might say something like this:
  Research amongst students in higher education in Europe and Australia reveals that students commonly adopt one of two approaches to learning. Those using the surface approach seem to focus their attention on isolated details. They try to memorize these individual details in the same form in which they first appeared. Those using the deep approach focus their attention on the underlying meaning or message. They attempt to relate their ideas together and construct their own meaning, possibly in relation to their own experience.

2   Ask the students:
See if you can identify the approach being taken by the students who made these statements:

    2.1   I don't like having to take notes in lectures. I like to be able to listen so that I can understand what the problem is. (Law student)

    2.2   I learn law by cases: listing cases and listing principles, I have a good short-term memory and I can memorize enough to get through examinations. (Law student)

    2.3   I read it. I read it very slowly, trying to concentrate on what it means. Obviously, I've read the quotations a few times and I've got it in my mind what they mean. I really try to read it slowly. There is a lot of meaning behind it. You have to really kind of get into it, and take every passage, every sentence, and try to really think, 'Well, what does this mean?' You mustn't regurgitate what David is saying because that's not the idea of the exercise, so I suppose it's really original ideas in this one, kind of getting it all together. (Geography student)

    2.4   Getting enough facts so that you can write something relevant in the exam. You've got enough information so you can write an essay on it. What I normally do is learn certain headings. I'll write a question down, about four or five different headings, which in an exam I can go: 'Introduction' and I'll look at the next heading and I know what I've got to write about without really thinking about it. I know the facts about it. I go to the next heading and regurgitate. (Computer Science Student)

(These statements derived from work undertaken at Oxford Brookes University by Professor Graham Gibbs (1992). The authors are grateful for his permission to include them.)

Your students should identify examples 2.1 and 2.3 as examples of the deep approach and examples 2.2 and 2.4 a examples of the surface approach. Discuss this as much as necessary, then tell them that examples 2.3 and 2.4 were direct quotations from the same student. In other words, this person was adopting a pragmatic (a so-called strategic) approach depending upon the context. In this case the Geography module required a deep approach and the Computer Science module a surface approach.

3   Then say to the students:
    I want you to work in pairs for this exercise.
    In your pairs:
- *identify areas of your current course (or modules) that lend themselves to a deep or a surface approach to learning (or to a combination of both);*
- *identify individual or pair group learning activities that can support either a deep or a surface approach to learning.*

(It will help to make the task clearer if you can display these instructions on the board, flip chart or the overhead projector.) Allow about 10 to 15 minutes for the pairs to work out some ideas.

4   Then debrief the class by leading a discussion in which you list the ideas from the students on the board, flip chart or on an overhead projector.

Guidelines for Receiving Peer Feedback

Students (and tutors) can experience considerable anxiety when their study or work tasks become overwhelming. This can happen when they receive assignments from several directions at once, or when they sometimes lose their focus or their sense of proportion. Asking for, and receiving peer feedback (whether you are a student or a tutor) can help you to regain your sense of purpose and perspective.

To achieve a balanced perspective we often need several sources of feedback to validate one another, so it is worth encouraging students to ask one another for help as well as their tutors.

How to Receive Feedback

To help students to make the most of the feedback they receive, take them through this checklist:

- Listen to and hear what is being said.
- Consider all the information that you are given. It is all too easy to disregard any information that is not what we expect or would like to hear.

- Avoid being defensive. It will inhibit the giving of all the relevant feedback. Listen to all that is being offered before responding.
- Always ask for clarification if you do not fully understand. Misunderstandings can inhibit the learning process.
- Think through and decide. Give yourself time to consider the feedback.
- Check it out if necessary by reference to another opinion or source.
- Assess its value and the implications of not addressing the issues or points that have been identified.
- Decide upon your strategy and seek help to undertake personal development if this is appropriate.

Chapter 2 Proformas

2.1 Introductions
2.2 Building Teams
2.3 Debriefing Phase/Feedback: Building Teams
2.4 Clarifying Students' Roles
2.5 Setting Ground Rules
2.6 Developing Your Skills of Reflection
2.7 Developing Your Awareness of Your Own Learning Styles and Methods

Introductions	Proforma 2.1

Setting the Scene
In this exercise the content of the discussion will remain within the group. You are encouraged to talk openly about yourselves but there is no compulsion to do so. Therefore, it is important to respect each others' information.

Working in Pairs
Divide into working pairs.
Each of you will interview your partner in turn for five minutes. The tutor will tell you when time is up

(If there is an odd number in the class then form a group of three)
The tutor will tell you when to start, when to change roles and when to finish.

Screening
At the end of the interview phase each member of the pair must check out with their partner if they disclosed any information during the interview which they do not wish other members of the group to know at this stage.

Feedback
Each member of each pair introduces his or her partner to the whole group, taking about two minutes each to do so or

Feedback (for groups of over 16)
Progress by 'snowballing':
Two pairs join together to form a quartet and each member of the pair introduces his or her partner in turn, taking about two minutes each.
(Time allocated for this phase, 10 minutes)
Proceed by 'snowballing' again, forming octets. Those in each octet then compile a list of the hobbies and interests that members have and elect a spokesperson.
(Time allocated 15 minutes)

Finally
The elected spokespersons introduce members of their octet to the whole group, and inform the whole group of the octet's interests.
(Time allocated n groups × 5 minutes)

Building Teams

Proforma 2.2

Setting the Scene
This activity will:

- enable you to get to know one another
- give you the opportunity to practise working in groups
- give you the opportunity to experience and reflect on group processes

For this activity you will work in teams of four, five or six.

Equipment
Each team will need the following equipment:

- a watch
- pens and large sheets of paper, e.g. flip chart paper
- scissors, string and glue

The Task of Each Team

- Design a game, using the materials supplied.
- Provide a player to play each game designed by the other groups.
- Design a method of evaluating the game for use once it has been played.

Game Design
The task of each team is to:

- appoint a team leader;
- design and manufacture the necessary materials to enable the game to be played;
- design and produce materials as necessary to be used by the team leader to evaluate the game once all games have been played.

You have 30 minutes for this activity

Playing the Games

- Teams provide volunteers to form groups to demonstrate each of the games created (NB: all evaluations will be carried out simultaneously when all the games have been played. Volunteers can play only one game each).
- Each team leader in turn selects and instructs a volunteer group how to play the game.
- Observers or other group members keep time and indicate when time is up.
- Each game is played in turn.
- Team leaders carry out an evaluation with the participants of their game, using the evaluation methods devised by their teams.

© Falmer Press

**Debriefing Phase/Feedback:
Building Teams**
Proforma 2.3

The tutor will lead the discussion on the processes which occurred throughout the activity.
Topics for discussion might include:

- How did the team members set about the task?
- Did you set initial ground rules?
- What roles emerged?
- Were these roles necessary in order to complete the activity?
- How were the roles assigned/assumed?
- How were decisions made?
- Was the activity achieved in the given time?
- How did you feel about being part of a group?
- What advantages are there in using team work for a task?
- How did volunteers feel about the game?

Use the space below to sum up the key points from the discussion.

Comment how the activity itself related to the aims set at the beginning of the session.

Personal Perspective
Use the space below to identify what you have learnt from this activity.

© Falmer Press

Clarifying Students' Roles   Proforma 2.4

Setting the Scene
The tutor will:

- introduce the session and explain why clarifying roles and responsibilities is of importance in learning;
- explore the course guide/student handbook and, in the case of a module or unit of study, move on to the briefing/descriptor and identify the content to be covered and the assessment component;
- clarify his or her role as a tutor;
- help you to identify your roles and responsibilities as students.

Identifying Your Roles and Responsibilities as Students
On your own generate ideas on the student role and responsibilities. (5 minutes) Then form small groups (of 4–5) and combine these ideas. (10 minutes)

Combine these ideas in the group to form a group list.
Each group nominates a reporter.

Each group in turn provides an idea for discussion by the class as a whole. A common list of roles and responsibilities is then mutually agreed.

NB: Where there are large numbers, the tutor will use the snowball technique where two groups meet to combine all their ideas in a common list, then two more groups merge and so on. The final list can be confirmed by the tutor.

Setting Ground Rules   Proforma 2.5

So that we can work together effectively as a group, it is important that we identify both our expectations from the course/module and the basis on which we are going to work.

On your own write down the answers to these questions:

- Why are you here?
- What do you hope to achieve by attending these sessions?
- What do you think your role in class should be?
- What is acceptable behaviour of other members of the class in terms of participation and attendance?
- What can you expect of the tutor?
- What would be the best way to handle sabotage?

You have five minutes for this task.

In pairs, share your ideas and discuss the similarities and differences between them. You have five minutes for this task.

In groups of four:

- appoint a scribe and agree a common list of ground rules for the future conduct of this class;
- write them on an acetate sheet for the overhead projector (or a sheet of flip chart paper).

You have 10 minutes for this task.

Each group will be asked to report back. Together we will select the common elements from the list and adopt these as the ground rules for the class.

Write your list of agreed ground rules here:

| **Developing Your Skills of Reflection** | Proforma 2.6 |

The following exercise is designed to help you to realize that the art of reflection lies in the process of systematic review of events and experiences to assist in the learning process. It enables us to be more prepared for the future. To reflect is not merely to commit a moment's thought, but to commit to an extended process.

1 *Think of a stressful event or experience connected with your recent academic work. Recall what happened in as much detail as you can.*

2 *Share this with a partner. Help one another to identify key issues and critical incidents by asking questions to encourage your partner to explore and expand their recall. You might do this best by focusing on contributory factors, and asking questions such as 'What happened next?', 'What was the result?'*

3 *Explore the underlying factors by asking questions about the feelings, attitudes and actions that were part of the event, and write your comments below.*

4 *Acknowledge the underlying principles and relate the theory to the actual event experience. For instance, can you identify accepted principles or received wisdom that sheds positive light on what happened, such as the theory on defence mechanisms, group dynamics, physiological symptoms of stress?*

5 Strategies for the future
Describe how you would like to deal with a similar situation if you are confronted with one in future. Are there any strategies that would help you to build up your personal resources to help you cope better in future?

Developing Your Awareness of Your Own Learning Methods and Styles Proforma 2.7

Research amongst students in higher education in Europe and Australia reveals that students commonly adopt one of two approaches to learning. Those using the surface approach seem to focus their attention on isolated details. They try to memorize these individual details in the same form in which they first appeared. Those using the deep approach focus their attention on the underlying meaning or message. They attempt to relate their ideas together and construct their own meaning, possibly in relation to their own experience.

On your own, see if you can identify the approach being taken by the students who made these statements:

1. I don't like having to take notes in lectures. I like to be able to listen so that I can understand what the problems is. (Law student)

2. I learn law by cases: listing cases and listing principles, I have a good short term memory and I can memorize enough to get through examinations. (Law student)

3. I read it. I read it very slowly, trying to concentrate on what it means. Obviously, I've read the quotations a few times and I've got it in my mind what they mean. I really try to read it slowly. There is a lot of meaning behind it. You have to really kind of get into it, and take every passage, every sentence, and try to really think, 'well, what does this mean?' You mustn't regurgitate what David is saying because that's not the idea of the exercise, so I suppose it's really original ideas in this one, kind of getting it all together. (Geography student)

4. Getting enough facts so that you can write something relevant in the exam. You've got enough information so you can write an essay on it. What I normally do is learn certain headings. I'll write a question down, about four or five different headings, which in an exam I can go: 'Introduction' and I'll look at the next heading and I know what I've got to write about without really thinking about it. I know the facts about it. I go to the next heading and regurgitate. (Computer Science Student)

(These statements derived from work undertaken at Oxford Brookes University by Professor Graham Gibbs. The authors are grateful for his permission to include them.)

In pairs, discuss your opinions and try to resolve any differences.
You have 5 minutes. Then your tutor will draw the discussions together and confirm which are which.
In your pairs:

- identify areas of your current course (or modules) that lend themselves to a deep or a surface approach to learning (or to a combination of both)
- identify individual or pair group learning activities that can support either a deep or a surface approach to learning. You have 10 minutes.

Your tutor will then debrief the class by leading a discussion in which he or she lists your ideas on the board, flip chart or on an overhead projector.

Chapter 3

Managing the Learning Experience by Academic Support Strategies

Some attention was given in the previous chapter to establishing a positive climate in the classroom as an essential framework for active learning. It is this climate that frequently becomes the litmus for the feelings of tension, anxiety and pressure.

Within student groups there are several positive strategies that can be implemented to ensure that students have a sense of direction and support in their studies. Such measures can help to dissipate the underlying feelings induced by pressure that can cause discomfort and barriers to learning. Tutors can use these practical approaches to support and sustain interaction with individual students or within groups.

Using Learning Agreements for Effective Group Work

Whilst group work is a collaborative and supportive way for students to undertake academic tasks they can feel varying degrees of pressure as they try to form and work in a team. This in turn can increase demands on the tutor. He or she can be called on to:

- resolve tensions in individuals and the group;
- satisfy group needs for information and support;
- assist in negotiating individuals' contributions;
- clarify roles.

In addition, there can be difficulties in managing group work because students can be unclear about what is expected in terms of coverage, volume and quality.

One way to approach this is to ask each group to compile a learning agreement that summarizes what they are going to do.

It is important to emphasize to students that any learning agreement will be an evolutionary document, so that it can change as the group's perception or nature of their task changes. Thus, the learning agreement proforma can incorporate space for updates and amendments to be agreed at an interim stage and signed by the students and if necessary, the tutor.

For a good introduction to learning agreements and contracts, see Bond (1988). (Remember that it is necessary to introduce students to the group and teamwork skills for them to manage their group work successfully.)

Sample Group Learning Agreement

Names of Group Members:

Group Project Title:

Date:

Project Brief:

1 What we plan to do in this project

2 What we intend to do to achieve our goals

3 Describe the form the final project will take, e.g. videotape, written report, a model, etc.

4 The roles and responsibilities that we have identified

5 How we intend to divide up the roles and responsibilities

6 Our own criteria for success and how we shall achieve them

7 Ways in which it will meet the criteria we have set

8 Possible problems and how we think we can tackle them

9 Amendments (after consultation with tutor)

Signed (Group members):

Signed (Tutor)

Grouping Students for Academic Tutorials

When there were fewer students it used to be feasible to have an open door policy for tutorial support. The increase in student numbers has made this impossible for most tutors. It can be very frustrating and potentially disruptive when large numbers of students come singly for help, each with the same problem.

To get over this difficulty, allow time in your schedule for a single meeting long enough to discuss the problem with a small group. It might even be worth booking a room for the meeting if your office is shared, or if there is only space in it for one or two people besides yourself. Then, when students present themselves singly for help with the particular problem you can say to them: *There will be a group tutorial on this problem at (say) 1.30 p.m. on (say) Thursday.*

In this way, you can save a lot of time because you will only have to deal with that particular issue on the one occasion, instead of repeating yourself for each student.

There are several additional advantages in this approach:

- you provide consistent information and support for each student with the same difficulty;
- you can be more prepared for a planned meeting, rather than several *ad hoc* tutorials;
- you can prepare special support material — if required;
- you can often lead students to resolve their own problem for themselves.

By keeping a record of each group tutorial that you run for the students, you can either plan ahead the following year and even issue the announcement in class about when and where they will take place — or you can teach the topic differently in the light of your experience in the tutorial the previous year, so that the students do not have that problem again.

Making Appointments for Personal Tutorials to Discuss Academic Progress

One of the consequences of the increase in student numbers has been the decline or disappearance of personal tutorials. Many tutors recognize that this was a worthwhile system and make valiant efforts to continue some sort of similar support despite the prevailing pressures to use their time for marking, administration and research.

Modular schemes mean that such provision is even more necessary for many students, particularly those whose programmes are not focused on a single discipline. Instead of trying to keep an open door for personal tutorials on demand, an alternative is to post a notice divided into 15 or 30 minute time slots during the week when it will be convenient for the tutor to see students. It is then the students' responsibility to sign in for the slot that they prefer, and to turn up on time. In this way the students do get a chance to see their tutor occasionally. We have to accept that demand might outstrip the supply of time available. However, this is better than no system at all.

Being a Consultant to Students Outside Contact Time

It is not always obvious to students that tutors have a defined area of academic expertise within their own discipline. Therefore, they tend to make inappropriate requests for help on academic matters. When this occurs frequently, it can increase tutors' stress levels by sapping their energy and pushing them towards the limits of their resources.

Each of us is a specialist in a given area and it is important to let students know exactly where we are prepared to advise and where other colleagues should be consulted. This is best undertaken collectively by the course team (or a similar group of tutors) each identifying clearly for students their area of expertise and research interest. It should also be made plain to students that matters of course administration are usually best handled by the appropriate support staff and not tutors. Reminders about this can be placed in the Student Handbook and posted on notice boards or diagramatically represented in a quick and easy reference chart.

Adopting Resource Based Learning (RBL)

Many universities and colleges are cutting back on the teaching time that they can allow in a course or a module. This puts tutors under increased pressure to try to cover the syllabus in less and less teaching time and this can increase the pressure within the learning environment, which in turn can create greater stress and anxiety for both tutors and students.

Resource based learning offers the opportunity for tutors to reappraise the way they interpret the syllabus and the means of providing appropriate learning experiences for their students. It involves the provision of learning resources, usually print, to enable students to learn more independently than has been normal in the past. The last thing tutors under pressure ought to do is to write a new text book or extensive learning materials on their own. It is better by far to adopt or adapt existing materials. One way of ensuring that students retain access to a source of high quality information is to write a study guide to an existing text. This gives them a firm base for their studies.

The tutor is then free to select the most appropriate teaching methods that guide and reinforce students' learning and that also give him or her the greatest personal satisfaction as a tutor. This could be an enhanced seminar programme, or intensive group project activities, or case studies, for instance. There might be a requirement for students to make presentations to one another and the tutor on the basis of their findings, or even the opportunity for some tutorial work with very small numbers of students in each session. This can be a lifeline for tutors who find facing very large groups either unsatisfactory educationally, or even intimidating.

Such an approach can only occur after detailed thought and planning to identify and enhance the best learning material to support students. Time spent at the early stage is an investment for successful implementation. There are several steps you can take to avoid potential pitfalls, for instance:

Introduce students carefully into this mode of learning
The traditional lecture and seminar/tutorial approach is generally accepted by students, and they can react adversely to changes for which they are not adequately prepared. An introductory session (or sessions) in which they are introduced to the materials, the style of the new course, the skills they will need to deploy for success, and expectations you have of them, is essential.

Give students frequent feedback on their progress
If students are to maintain their interest and motivation on a course of study, careful thought needs to be given as to how this is to be provided on a resource based course: for example, short answer quizzes in seminars, peer feedback, work sheets with answers in sealed packs attached for students to open when they wish to check the accuracy of their work.

Help students to retain a feeling of belonging to a course or module
This is important because they may spend a lot less time with the

tutor, and more time studying alone or in small groups. Experience has shown that abandoning lectures entirely can be a big mistake. Perhaps the nature of the lecture needs to change, so that it becomes much more of a sign posting and problem solving session, rather than a vehicle for transmitting the information students have already in their learning resources. It seems that a large proportion of students value the social act of being together in lectures with the tutor, and it helps to give them a sense of belonging.

Ensure that any text book that you decide to use will not be withdrawn from publication abruptly
This can destroy the best laid plans for resource based learning. It might be worth contacting the publisher of any text that you select as the basis of a resource based learning course to make sure that the book will remain in print long enough to justify your efforts.

Get the help and advice of at least one colleague
This can be invaluable as you create the new learning material for students. Colleagues are often a very good source of support and ideas when the going gets tough and they can often think of approaches and ideas that enhance the original concept.

Get the support of your course tutor or programme manger for the changes you wish to make
This should be an essential requirement before making a start on any move to resource based learning because it might be necessary to obtain formal academic approval for these changes. It might also be possible to get a commitment to allow you to run the course or module yourself for a few iterations so that you recoup the benefit of the extra time you put in. You might need to obtain the extra finance to cover photocopying or print costs which are likely to be greater than those for a traditional course.

Conduct an evaluation of how the course is going at an early interim stage
This can help you to identify problems before they get too big to handle. It can also help you to fine tune your new course to make sure that students get the maximum benefit from the experience. For this evaluation, you might wish to interview students yourself, or to use a feedback questionnaire or to enlist the help of your educational development unit, if your college has one.

NB If you decide to produce RBL materials, it is vital to observe the current copyright legislation and protocols. Your librarian will advise you.

Giving Telephone Tutorials

Being separated from the university or college and the course can be a stressful experience for students, and it can also be hard work for the tutor to keep in touch with such students on a planned and coherent basis. Nevertheless, occasions can arise where it is important for a student to remain in touch with the course even though they are living off campus and are unable to travel in for face-to-face meetings. This could be because of illness, or because they are on work or sandwich placement, for example. Whatever the reason, it is important that, as the tutor, you retain contact with the student, and keep the student in contact with the academic life of the course.

This can often best be done by using the telephone, although running a telephone tutorial can be a tiring business, particularly if it is protracted. This is partly because on the telephone there are none of the normal non-verbal cues that normally lubricate face-to-face conversations. Thus it is important not to plan to cover too much ground on one session on the telephone. This ensures that fatigue does not set in. It can also allow the student to assimilate and reflect on the discussion.

It will also help both you and the students if you have a plan, or agenda, that both of you can see and share. This gives structure to the transaction and might give you the opportunity to set a time for each item to ensure that the session doesn't go on too long. (Where a student is a long way overseas so that their waking times and yours do not easily coincide, then it might be more appropriate to use E-mail tutorials.)

Giving E-mail Tutorials

When time is at a premium, it can be very useful to:

- defer certain activities until there is time to give them your full attention;
- prioritize work commitments.

This can prevent further overloading which is stressful.

With the videotape recorder has come the idea of 'time shift' — recording the programme during an otherwise busy time for replay later. Now, with the general availability of computers, networks and electronic mail (E-mail) to students and staff, so comes the concept of E-main tutorials. Instead of face-to-face tutorials it is now possible to conduct one to one or even group tutorials via the computer terminal on your desk.

Tutors who operate tutorials in this way report that another advantage is that students seem to take much more care when writing questions and responses than they tend to do when talking face-to-face.

How to Run the E-mail Tutorials

- Ensure that you have a reliable connection from your computer or terminal to the University or College network, and that the students do too.
- Exchange E-mail addresses with them.
- Write a question or topic for discussion to each of them. (This can be the same message, dispensed to all students at a single keystroke, if you have a group facility on your network, or it can be the same or a different message dispatched separately to each student.)
- Make it clear in the message that you expect a reply by a certain date (and time, if appropriate).
- As you receive the replies you can compose your responses to them and send them to individual students or to the group as a whole.
- Allow the dialogue to continue for as many exchanges of message as you wish.

The process has an added advantage in that you do not need to confine yourself to corresponding in this way with students within the institution. You can use exactly the same mechanism to exchange messages with students elsewhere — provided you each have access to the necessary equipment, software and electronic network.

Running Self-help Groups and Networks

Students often find themselves on individual pathways within a course, in large or very large groups of strangers who might remain strangers even after several months. Such students can feel socially and academically isolated and deprived of a shared purpose. In these circumstances, their perceptions of their academic difficulties can become disproportionate and support from peers might not be forthcoming immediately.

Self help groups can be set up to fulfil an important social and academic purpose. These can spontaneously evolve to meet a special interest or need. In the early days of a module or course of study it will probably be helpful to encourage students to form support networks and self help groups. Such groups can:

- establish a collegial spirit;
- have very practical, task-oriented functions for handling the learning aspects of the course. For example, students in such groups might share texts to enable them to cover a wider variety of sources of information than would be available to an individual;
- help in understanding difficult theoretical concepts or for sharing information, or in consolidation or revision tasks.

A formal arrangement for helping students to do this in difficult subject areas in particular is detailed in 'Supplemental Instruction', Wallace (1996). This takes resources and is a more formal and, in the USA, is a proven way of supporting students in their studies. Successful students from the previous year's course or module are trained and paid to lead study groups on a regular basis. The essence of the operation is that they are facilitators not tutors. This approach does require additional resources. However, particularly in the USA it is a proven way of making consistent, measurable positive effects on students' attainment (Rust and Wallace, 1994).

Initially, as with any groups to be formed, groups' members need to get to know one another, and to set the ground rules upon which the group will operate. Initially, the tutor might need to book a room for these regular meetings, but once these groups are established, then he or she can withdraw allowing them the full freedom to steer their own course. The success of such groups often depends upon a shared sense of purpose and the commitment of the individual members interacting as a group.

Developing Your Students' and Your Own Self-Management and Learning Skills

Part of becoming an effective student, or an effective tutor involves being in control of oneself, one's time and one's relationship with others — or at least feeling that you have this control most of the time. These practical ideas, like many in the rest of the book are written in a form for use with student groups. With some modification, several might also be helpful for tutors to use in work with their colleagues.

Relaxation

Relaxation is one of the best antidotes to stress. Students who have difficulty concentrating during the day or sleeping at night can benefit from learning relaxation techniques. Students who suffer from panic attacks or other forms of anxiety can learn to stay in control by relaxing and slowing down their breathing. All students who have to sit in class or at their desks for long periods will be more alert and more centred and calm if they introduce short periods of relaxation into their routine.

Even where classes are meeting for the first session of the day, it can be very useful to begin with a short exercise in relaxation or aerobics, or to introduce one as a 'break' at some point in the session. When the class is merely the latest in a tedious day-long schedule then it can be indispensable. Gradually, it should be possible for students to build up a repertoire of relaxation exercises they can use, not only in class, but whenever they want: before an examination, for instance, or when they return to their room or lodgings at the end of the day.

How to run the activity: Relaxation

(This exercise is written in the form of a script for the tutor to read to the class.)

I am going to take you through a relaxation routine known as progressive muscular relaxation. If you haven't done this kind of thing before it might take you a little while to become familiar with the routine. But I am sure that if you give it a go you will feel the benefit. The routine will only take 5 minutes.

Put aside your pens, books and notes. Sit upright in your seat, in a way that is comfortable for you. Close your eyes, if you wish to do so. Put your hands on your thighs. Take a deep breath, and hold it whilst I count to five: one, two, three, four, five. And now breathe out gradually.

Take another deep breath in and, this time, tense the muscles of your feet and ankles. Hold it for a count of five. One, two, three, four, five. Now, as you breathe out, gradually relax these muscles.

Now breathe in again slowly and tense your calves and thighs. Hold it for a count of five. One, two, three, four, five. As you breathe out, gradually relax these muscles, and feel the tension flowing out of your muscles as they relax slowly.

Repeat these instructions with the following groups of muscles: abdomen and lower back, chest and neck, arms and shoulders, face and scalp. Bring the exercise to a close with the following words:
Now take two minutes to relax in silence and think about something that gives you pleasure. (Wait two minutes.) *Now take a minute to think about today.* Wait one minute *Now let us begin our work.*

It is likely that some students will feel embarrassed or uncooperative when you first suggest these exercises but, with time, everyone will come to enjoy them and even to look forward to them. They only take a few minutes and make an excellent prelude to exercises which encourage reflection. For students who find this particularly beneficial there is a number of texts that take a deeper approach to relaxation. It is important that students feel at ease with a technique both physically and emotionally (see Mitchell (1987)).

Using Aerobics

Even though there is a trend towards fewer class contact hours, students sometimes spend extended periods, even whole days, sitting in class. This relentless pressure inevitably leads to restlessness, drowsiness and loss of concentration. They sit for many hours in cramped, ill ventilated surroundings, often with little chance to move — not unlike airline passengers. Several airlines now play aerobics videotapes for their passengers to participate in towards the end of long-haul flights. They recognize that some form of physical activity is needed to help their passengers recover from sitting in these circumstances for long periods. The effects are invigorating and enjoyable. What is necessary and possible in an airline seat can also be necessary and possible in classrooms.

How to run the activity: Using Aerobics

(The following activity should be introduced positively to students and the rationale for its use explained.)

The tutor might introduce the activity by saying:
It is obvious that you have been sitting passively for a long time today. Let us spend a few minutes loosening up physically. Here are some simple exercises you can do whilst sitting in your seats. Put your book and pens on one side, and follow me.

Sit on a chair in full view of everyone in the class, and switch on the tape recorder (if you have one) with some 'bouncy' music to help everyone keep together. Say loudly and energetically,
We will start by simple leg raising. Lift each foot in turn a few inches off the floor in time to the music. Demonstrate as you give the instructions.

Next introduce some (limited) arm and hand movements. Say, and demonstrate,
Now raise your arms straight above you and, in time to the music, bring each hand in turn down level with your shoulder. (This should be manageable even in the most restricted tiered lecture theatre). Continue this for a few moments and then introduce variations, using opposing sets of muscles to provide exercise in these restricted conditions. For instance, you might say,
Now stop that exercise and try this one. Place both your hands on top of one thigh (demonstrate as you speak). *Now press down with your hands and push up with your thigh.* Allow your thigh to move up in a controlled and limited way a few times. *Now try the other thigh.* Repeat the exercise.

If there is room you might also want to try the following as a further variation:
Place your left hand against your right forearm. Push down with your arm against resistance from your hand. Do this four or five times, saying *You can make this as hard or as easy for yourself as your like by increasing or reducing the resistance that you apply with your hand.*

Developing Time Management Skills

One of the most stressful experiences for students (and tutors) can be the feeling that the various aspects of life are out of control. This is often related to excessive workload or being over committed. The use of diaries and Filofax systems is a starting point. These can be used to identify tasks and timescales from which to work. A more effective strategy is to develop skills to manage time and to prevent overload. This might mean that more work can be accomplished in the time available or that through prioritizing, some of the least important items can be ignored or postponed. The following exercise gives students the chance to practice organizing time in a simulation.

How to run the activity: Developing Time Management Skills

Explain to the students that this exercise simulates a situation that a typical student is likely to find themselves in on a Thursday in February. They are to make (or use) the blank hourly timetable form for each day for Friday, Saturday Sunday and Monday to plan their time to cope with the situation in which they find themselves. Give them 30 minutes to perform the task. Use Proformas 4.1–4.6 of daily planners on pp. 62–8.

Events and Tasks

You have had a bad toothache on and off since yesterday morning.

Saturday is a relative's birthday. You have not bought a card or present.

You have not phoned, written or visited home since Christmas.

There is the chance of a job a couple of evenings a week, but you would have to go and see someone about it either this evening or tomorrow evening.

There is a Horizon programme on TV tomorrow evening at 8pm which your tutors feel is very relevant to the work you are doing at present.

Tonight's TV schedule includes as usual *Neighbours, Home and Away* and *Coronation Street.* Tomorrow is much the same, but there is also *Top of the Pops* and *EastEnders.*

You have a book out of the library which is due back tomorrow.

You have been invited to a friend's in London this weekend. You will need to pack and make travel arrangements.

You need to photocopy an assignment before you hand it in on Friday.

You have a lab session from 2.00–4.00 tomorrow.

You owe someone £10 and they will be in your 2.00–4.00 lab tomorrow.

Remember you have to travel to and from university.

You have a lecture and seminar tomorrow from 9.00–11.00.

Your personal tutor has put up a note asking to see you as soon as possible.

You have no clean underwear left!

It would be advisable to eat and shower at some time.

You have been assigned a group project — the group has arranged to meet at 6pm tomorrow for one hour.

You need to get some money from somewhere — you only have 89p on you.

Everyone is going out for a drink tonight.

You missed a lecture last week — it might be advisable to copy up the notes before the class on Monday.

You did not finish all the work in the lab session yesterday — it needs to be done before next week.

A friend wrote to you four weeks ago — it is your turn to write or phone.

A major assignment is due in at 9am on Monday morning. You have not yet done the library research, the writing and the word-processing. This will take up to 15 hours of work, and you will lose 5 per cent of your mark each day it is late.

You have invited your lover round for a candle lit dinner tomorrow evening. There is no food (or anything else) in the house!

You have a mid-sessional exam in three weeks' time.

Reflection

Debrief them as follows:

Whether we are aware of it or not, we make decisions about how to use our time on the basis of our values and goals.

Goals

Goals are our ambitions and desires — what we want to achieve. Goals should spring directly from our values. If not, we are unlikely to attain that particular goal, since we shall be working against ourselves. Goals cannot usually be achieved by a single action alone, but usually take time and many activities before they are realized.

Maintenance, Progress, Urgent and Important Tasks

Maintenance tasks are those that are essential to our everyday functioning, like washing, eating, sleeping. Progress tasks are those that get us nearer to our goals, such as studying, completing assignments, and so on. Urgent tasks are those that need to be done in the next few hours or so, important tasks are those that need to be done at some time, but not necessarily immediately. Coping with urgent, maintenance tasks can often mean that the important progress tasks do not get done.

In planning our time, we make conscious or unconscious decisions based upon our values and goals. The ways in which each of you chose to spend the weekend in this simulation was based upon these inmost feelings about what is important. It can be very helpful to be clear about our priorities and to make sure that we address these in disposing of our time. It can also be essential to plan ahead to make sure that priority items do not become impossible to cover.

Put these definitions on the overhead projector, or make them available as a handout (Proforma 4.7 is included on p. 69). Say to the students

I should like you to reflect on the process of decision-making, and the process of deciding priorities. The following questions might help you to think about these matters:

What did you decide to do, and what not to do?
What does this tell you about your goals and priorities?
To what extent are you influenced by external factors?

Then ask the students to make a second timetable or hand out pre-printed copies and say:

On this second timetable, make a real monthly plan for yourselves, thinking about what you have learned from this exercise. Photocopiable Proforma 4.8 of monthly planners on pp. 70–1.

Then introduce some ideas about the use of a diary or Filofax.

(The authors would like to thank Sandra Prince of the School in Mathematics and Information Sciences at Coventry University for the exercises used in this item.)

Balancing Lifestyle

'All work and no play'. . . Establishing a healthy lifestyle is important for everyone in higher and further education. The pace of institutional life has increased dramatically over recent years. Life no longer focuses on 30 weeks of three terms; it appears to be 52 weeks, particularly for the increasing number of students who need to work to support themselves.

Increasingly students have much 'baggage' with them as they work through their education (loans, pressure of work, need for paid employment to supplement their grant). In addition, mature students have dependents; these are not only children but parents in need of care. This has translated into a hidden workload with the increased need for pastoral care. Tutors are advised to refer students with specific problems/issues/needs which require resolution to trained student counsellors.

It is, however, our responsibility as tutors to highlight to all students the need for them to keep a perspective on life; a balanced lifestyle and in particular 'time out' or space at high pressure points in the year. (For many tutors, too, it appears that work roles are in overload, with role expectations exceeding their nature or limits. Bearing in mind the issue of student and work problems in the context of a healthy lifestyle, it is essential that we as tutors observe the code of professional distancing, by leaving the issues of work at work.)

An exercise that tutors can use with their students (and do in private for themselves) is as follows.

How to run the activity: Balancing Lifestyle

Say to the students:
We all need to be mindful that there is a balance in life which enables us to remain healthy and interesting individuals who can enjoy all that life has to offer.
It is crucial that you remind yourselves of dimensions of your life besides your academic work. A healthy lifestyle is about having a comfortable balance between work, leisure and life roles. Supportive of a healthy lifestyle are the following: sufficient sleep, a balanced diet and physical fitness.

Present the class with the following questions, either orally, or on the overhead projector or on a handout. A photocopiable Proforma 4.9 is included on p. 72.

Do you have the right balance between the time you give to work, recreation, and other activities?

Would you like to spend more time on activities that keep you fit and healthy?

Do you spend as much time as you would like with family and friends?

Then ask your students to complete the following chart.

Achieving balance — Assessment

At present I rate the quality of my life as follows:

	Poor	Adequate	Good	Excellent
Work				
Sleep (amount and quality)				
Social Life				
Leisure and Hobbies				
Health and Exercise				
Self Development e.g. acquisition of personal or professional skills and qualifications				

To bring the activity to a close, ask the students to think of an action plan — ideas of how to achieve a better balance and how they might implement their plans.

Developing Listening Skills

When we are tired, anxious and/or under pressure the 'listening and hearing' process which we normally engage in becomes less effective even to the point of being faulty. This leads to misinterpretations of the content and possibly the context of the communication. The consequences may be that anxiety, perplexity and confusion are increased and/or that conflict may arise. All of these are potential sources of stress.

How to run the activity: Developing Listening Skills

Before you introduce the concept of active listening skills, explain to the student group why such skills are important in our personal communication. Using an overhead projector, talk through how problems commonly arise in communications, see Burton and Dimbleby (1995), or ask the students to generate some examples in buzz groups.

Common problems in listening can arise from:
- Merely taking note of the information and content and not taking note of the context and feeling behind it.
- Allowing ourselves to be distracted and side-tracked into our own interests, which often leads us to hearing only what we wanted to hear.
- Being put off by the context of the message, or by extraneous factors.
- Preparing our response before the speaker has finished.
- Not looking as if we're listening, i.e. failing to give verbal and non-verbal feedback to the speaker. (Burton and Dimbleby, 1995)

Then give the students a handout (see pp. 73–4 for Proforma 4.10) with the following information on it and talk them through it, leading discussion to clear up any difficulties.

We are going to examine the component parts of the process of listening and how we can be more aware of potential difficulties.

Let us consider listening. It is part of the two way communication process which requires the individual to:

- *attend to the speaker;*
- *actively listen to the content of linguistic aspects of communication — speech;*
- *be aware of the paralinguistics — the timing, tone, accent and volume of speech.*

We also need to note that non-verbal behaviour or body language can be indicators of the individual's feelings associated with the context of the spoken word or the context in which the communication has arisen or is arising. We need to be aware of this component of communication from our own perspective and ask the question: What am I going to convey to others? What strategies can we implement to minimize stress and avoid conveying inaccurate messages?

Attending

We need to develop skills in focusing in on the communication partner; by setting aside our preoccupations during the communication. This 'baggage' interferes with the clarity of our thoughts about the communication itself. Unless we can discard it, it can block our responses within the process and distract us from the necessary observations.

Active observation

In addition we need to practise active observation. The process of communication requires us to notice several aspects of the communication partner as detailed above. You can practise active observation outside the communication process, to develop your skills.

Listening

In this part of the process we need to engage in active listening strategies. Merely catching a message is not sufficient. We need to process the content of the message and 'hear' what and how it is being said. To hear and be fully aware of the message conveyed is to note the content of what is being said, the way it is being said and the feelings behind the communication itself.

Reflecting

Reflecting on critical communications in terms of what we engage in and retain is a helpful way forward in developing listening skills. Begin to use checking out techniques as ways of ensuring that you have grasped the key issues/components of the communication.

- *Ask your partner within the communication to repeat/summarize key points.*
- *Reflect back your understanding as a form of summarizing.*
- *Ask for clarification.*
- *Ask for time to think through the essence of the conversation if you are being asked to make a decision/action which you are not comfortable with.*

In releasing the 'baggage' we hold for the period of the communication we are enabling ourselves to 'focus in' and engage in the process. In listening we also need to resist the temptation to think ahead to the next question and or rehearse the next sequence, as this inhibits our full engagement.

If the communication is a planned event then a rehearsal phase can be preparation for the dialogue. You can think through and check

*out key questions and or areas which must be included. This is par-
ticularly helpful if the planned communication is likely to be difficult
in some way.*

*Listening and hearing in a busy environment is an art, and as such
is one which we must all practise. Much can be gained from reflecting
upon one's approach to the activity and setting a goal to develop the
skills; for effective listening skills can save time, place you under less
pressure and boost your confidence when you 'hear' the positives in the
conveyance of a message. Passive listening means you miss out: active
listening means you stay informed and in tune.*

Developing Presentation Skills

Many students find that the prospect of having to make an oral presentation is very threatening, whether they are due to perform alone or in
groups. Sometimes the anxiety can be so severe that individuals become physically ill — so nervous that it inhibits clear thoughts and
effective delivery. One way to alleviate this tendency in students is to
give them practice before hand.

How to run the activity: Developing Presentation Skills

Explain to the students that this exercise is practice to allow them to
develop some of the necessary skills prior to their formal assessed
presentations. Hand out the Proforma 4.11 on p. 75.

Divide the class into group of four or five
Ask them to:

- Introduce themselves to their neighbours/other group members.
- Generate a list of factors that they think are important in planning and delivering good presentations
- Put them into an agreed order of priority, listing the most important first and so on.

Preparing a presentation
Then ask the groups of four/five to prepare a five minute presentation
on the factors which their group think are important in planning and
delivering a presentation.

Delivering an excellent presentation

Then ask each group in turn to make a five minute presentation on their own factors for excellent presentations. Each member of the group should make a more or less equal spoken contribution in the presentation to the larger group. The other groups should assess each group on the basis of their own criteria. Each group will be asked to give feedback to each presentation, on the basis of their own criteria. The Proforma on Peer Evaluation, 4.12 on pp. 76–8 can be used as a record.

Debriefing

When each group has made its presentation then you might wish to hand out the criteria for assessment that will be used in the class work assessment and discuss the following points (amongst others):

- eye contact
- posture
- use of the voice (pitch, volume, tone)
- clarity of visual displays
- the vital importance of rehearsal before the presentation

The whole exercise can take up to two hours, depending upon the size of your class. With very large classes, you might want to split the class into parallel sessions each supervised by a colleague. For further reference, students can be directed to texts on public speaking and presentations. A useful practical guide is Campbell (1990).

Developing Self Awareness

When under pressure or feeling stressed we become less alert to what is going on around us and less able to recognize our own actions and the implications and consequences of those actions.

Self-awareness is the process of attending to and noticing what we are doing. Self-awareness is therefore a process of self-monitoring; that is being focused on our actions, both verbal and non-verbal. An enhancement in this aspect of ourselves is of benefit in terms of being keyed into and alert to events and the context which surrounds them; in other words, you 'stay awake' (Burnard (1992)).

The self is a complex concept. Each of us has a public self and a private self. The public self is how others see us, our body and our behaviour (verbal and non-verbal). Therefore, in developing self awareness we need to recognize the feedback others offer or give/impose on us.

The private self refers to our feelings, thoughts and intuitions. If we do not reflect on these aspects of self then we deny ourselves the opportunity to learn from current experiences and therefore test/establish a strategy for handling the next experience more comfortably or effectively.

The development of self-awareness enhances not only personal skills; it can enhance the quality of interpersonal relationships, which is an intrinsically satisfying element of work and life roles. It can also help us to be more productive because, with it, we are more effective as people.

Activities to encourage self-awareness:

- Give students time to enter into the process of reflection.
- Encourage the use of journals and diaries in a reflective way, to note critical events and the feelings and thoughts surrounding them.
- Engage in the use of student presentations and student-led seminars where peer observation and feedback can be used to contribute as the feedback mechanism from significant others.
- Provide assertiveness skills training.
- Encourage students to consider a balanced lifestyle to include sporting activities that enhance the physical awareness of self in movement and activity.

The self is dynamic and changes depending on the external factors. A combination of these techniques to promote self-awareness is helpful. The greater degree of awareness we have the more strategies wc have as a way forward in resolving some of the aspects of life which are uncomfortable to live with.

Developing Assertiveness

One of the major contributors to work-related stress for both tutors and students is workload. Often as tutors we accept additional work at a time when we are already overburdened. In the same way, for instance, students passively accept an extra assignment at times when they are already struggling to complete work for other tutors as well as trying to keep up with their studies.

There is a phrase 'If you never say "no", what is your "yes" worth?' In other words, it behoves us all to be selective in the extra work we take on. Of course, a bald 'no' is unlikely to be acceptable, particularly from students to tutors, but there are ways of stating the current position quietly but firmly, and asking the other party to take this into account — the trait of assertiveness. Porritt (1990) defines assertive behaviour as

> . . . that which attends to and informs others of one's needs and feelings and sends the message to the other in such a way that neither person is belittled, put down or blamed.

This trait is not just appropriate at times in academic life, but applies to behaviour in other life roles.

As a means of increasing students' awareness of assertiveness, introduce the concept of assertive behaviour within the classroom setting.

How to run the activities: Developing Assertiveness

(NB: These activities work best with a class or group of students who have worked together successfully already.)

Introduction
Introduce the concept of assertiveness to students by saying:
There are times for all of us when it is necessary to assert our own needs within our peer group, at home and even to those in authority. There are different ways of going about this.

Then say to them:
There is a big difference between assertiveness and aggression, and between passive behaviour and assertiveness. The following activities are designed to introduce some ideas about assertiveness, and to give you some experience of how to say no.

What is assertiveness?
Introduce this activity by saying:
On your own, reflect on your understanding of assertive, aggressive, and passive behaviour. Write down examples that you have encountered.
(Allow 5 minutes)
In pairs or threes, share the experiences and reflections with your partners.
(Allow 10 minutes for this activity)
In groups of no more than six, appoint a reporter for the group. Write down some agreed definitions of assertiveness, aggressiveness and passive behaviour on poster paper or acetate, plus an example of each.
(Allow 15 minutes for this activity)

Give the groups poster paper, or acetates on which to write their conclusions.

Ask the group reporters to report back with comments, and draw attention to any key points they might have missed. The sort of key points you might wish to look for are:

- Assertive behaviour is characterized by directness, being outwardly expressive, taking responsibility, being inner directed, and letting the other person know how you feel. The assertive person does not blame or put down the other person.
- Aggressiveness is also characterized by being outwardly expressive and direct, letting the other person know how you feel, but also blames or puts down the other person, and avoids taking responsibility.
- Passive behaviour is characterized by inhibited action, concealing feelings from the other person, being other directed, and the avoidance of responsibility.

(Allow 3 minutes per group for this activity)

The Instant Replay Technique
Introduce this idea by saying:

When you are assertive, it is important that you do not capitulate. Therefore you need to use the Instant Replay Technique to make it clear that you are not prepared to give ground. To do this, simply repeat your request or position. For example you might say, over and over again in the face of repeated requests 'I am sorry, I am unable to do that'. 'I am sorry, I am unable to do that'.

You might wish to encourage the class to practise this together in the following exercises. To help students to develop the technique, you might say:

In real life encounters, it is often necessary to rephrase your initial statement or request to clarify your position.

Role Play Exercises

Exercise 1 Making a Request of a Friend

Say to the students:
Form groups of three. Choose one person who will make a request and one person who will refuse it. Make sure that you use the instant replay

technique (*repeating yourself, replaying the same phrase or position when being assertive*). *The third person will be an observer, looking at the behaviour of the other two.*

Say to the role play pairs:
The objective of the exercise is for each person to practise using the 'instant replay' technique. Each of you makes a request of the other. It might be to borrow money or to allow you to copy an essay, for instance. You are free to think up a suitable request. Then one person has three minutes to ask for the assistance he or she needs, and the other person has to practise saying 'No'. The person making the request can deploy as many verbal, logical and other devices as possible to try to make her/his partner agree. Then you change over.

Exercise 2 Asking for a Bigger Overdraft

Ask the students:
What assertive behaviour a student might use in asking a bank official for a further extension on their overdraft?

Lead the discussion that follows.

Then tell the students:
Form groups of three. Decide amongst yourselves who will play the bank official, who the student and who the observer.
Then hand out the following role briefs to the appropriate people before beginning the five minute exercise.

Introduce the exercise by saying:
The objective of the exercise is for each person to practise using the 'instant replay' technique. One of you plays the role of a student who wishes to borrow more money from the bank. You are free to think up suitable arguments to support your request. You have three minutes to ask for the assistance you need. The other person plays the role of the bank official, and has to practise saying 'No'. The person making the request can deploy as many verbal, logical and other devices as possible to try to make her/his partner agree. Then you change over.

Role Play: Role Brief Bank Official
Your role in the bank is to liaise with students about the operation of their accounts. There are in-house guidelines about the level of overdraft

you will permit a student to incur. For the purpose of this role play that limit is £2000. Under very exceptional circumstances, you do have discretion to increase this figure up to £2500, but experience has taught you that this tends to leave students in even greater difficulty in the long run, so you are very reluctant to allow this to happen. This is particularly so because you have a nineteen-year-old student in your family who is in their second year at university, who has already run up debts of £3000, and who is desperate to know how they are going to pay it off.

Role Play: Role Brief Student
You are in your second year at university/college. Your father (formerly a tutor) has taken early retirement on the grounds of ill health, and your mother has a part-time job as a receptionist in a doctor's surgery. They struggle to live on your father's pension and your mother's small income. They try to give you money to help you with your expenses, but you know it is difficult for them, and this leaves you dependent upon an inadequate grant — one on which it is not possible to live. You are at your overdraft limit of £2000 and you will not have enough money to pay your rent and food in two weeks' time unless you can persuade the bank official to increase your overdraft.

Conclude the exercise by saying:
I shall now ask each of the observers in turn to comment on what they observed in the role plays.

Lead the ensuing discussion and try to bring it to a neat close with a summary along these lines:
> *Assertiveness is not a guaranteed way of getting what you want. However, it can be a mature and effective way of opening negotiations. Before you begin, you need to make up your mind about what is the bottom line for you (the absolute minimum or maximum you will agree to) and stick to that through thick and thin. This could be a compromise position that you have worked out beforehand, or a fall back position. You will not normally reveal this in the early stages. Think beforehand what strategies you are going to adopt and what point you need to introduce during the conversation.*

Although this exercise is designed for tutors to use with students, it can work equally well amongst groups of colleagues who wish to develop their own assertiveness. (The authors would like to thank Sarah Williams of the Educational Development Unit at Coventry University for the role play exercises used in this item.)

Developing Problem Solving Skills (Including Brainstorming)

It can be very stressful for students to be suddenly confronted with the need to solve problems in an academic context without some help and preparation. A useful introduction to the subject can include the Nine Dot Problem (Rawlinson 1981).

How to run the activity: Nine Dot Problem

Give out the sheets with the nine dots problem on them.
Tell the students that:

- the task they have is to join the nine dots with four straight lines, without taking the pen or pencil off the paper;
- they should work silently on their own for 4 minutes.

After four minutes say:
Has anyone found the solution?
If someone thinks they have, ask them to explain to the rest of the class. If they are wrong or have only found a partial solution demonstrate the following on the board or overhead projector.

Step 1.

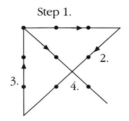

Follow this up with a discussion of lateral thinking — going outside the imagined boundaries of the problem. The only way to solve the nine dot problem is to think outside the frame imposed by the nine dots. Similarly, in creative problem solving, we need to think beyond the boundaries of conventional frames. You might then go on to introduce brainstorming.

(Similar exercises can be found in management training manuals.)

Developing Brainstorming Skills

As part of their academic studies, students are sometimes asked to work in groups to generate a novel solution to solve a problem. This can apply particularly in the design components of Art and Engineering, but it can also be part of courses or modules in Business, Environmental Studies and similar disciplines.

Without help and practise, this can be a formidable task, leading in some cases to frustration and anger. Brainstorming is a recognized tool for solving particular types of problems — those that require some innovative or lateral thinking. Tutors can help students to do this by giving them experience of a problem-solving technique, such as brainstorming, that they can apply in these circumstances.

How to run the activity: Brainstorming

Begin by saying something like this:
Soon you will be asked to work in groups to generate possible solutions to a problem. Today we are going to practise one technique that you will find helpful in doing this.
Form the students into groups (if you have not already done so).
Then say: *These are the problems that I want you to suggest solutions for today.*
Put up on the board or the overhead projector this list of problems (or ones like them that you have thought of):
Design an innovative method of assessment for this module that reflects the syllabus content and safeguards current standards.
Create a scheme for raising funds for either a local voluntary organization or the Students Union. The scheme must be able to attract helpers and have novel and new ideas to attract funds.
Then hand out the following guidelines for Brainstorming.

Brainstorming: Some Notes for Participants

Brainstorming is a technique for generating ideas or solutions which might not arise during a conventional committee or group meeting. Brainstorming works on the principle of spontaneous and uncensored contributions from participants.

It is appropriate only for attempts to solve the sorts of problems for which creative and innovative solutions are appropriate. Hence matters of knowledge or procedure, such as 'How do I place a small ad. in the paper?' are obviously inappropriate, whereas problems such as, 'What is the best use I can make of my old, broken down greenhouse?' might well lend themselves to brainstorming.
Step 1
Appoint a recorder. This person will write down an the chalkboard, flip chart or overhead projector, a list of all the suggestions from the members

of the group. This person is also able to make suggestions and add them to the list.

Step 2

Formulate the problem and write it on the chart/board/ohp as a reminder. In many ways this is the most crucial aspect of the procedure, and it is worth spending some time to make sure that the problem is stated in the best possible way.

Step 3

Members of the group think of possible (or not so possible) ideas and solutions and call them out. The recorder writes them down. An alternative is to give each student a pen, group them round a large piece of paper and allow them each to write their ideas as they think of them. (It can also be helpful to record the initials of the person who suggested it next to each idea.)

It is important that there should be no critical comments or evaluation at this stage. All suggestions have equal weight. Try to generate as may solutions as possible in the time available, and to make them as wild and unconventional as possible. It is this unconstrained, free approach which makes brainstorming potentially so valuable. It can also be helpful to try to build on previous suggestions.

Step 4

When you have run out of time or ideas, start to review and evaluate the suggestions. If necessary ask each person to explain their ideas in more detail. Isolate those which are worthy of implementation or further exploration.

Step 5

Revert to normal meeting mode and further develop the ideas you generated.

Talk the class through the process step by step, and then give them time in their groups to agree upon the problem that they are going to tackle using the technique of brainstorming.

Control the brainstorming process by moving groups on from stage to stage at intervals that you judge to be appropriate. At the end, ask a spokesperson from each group to report back on the solution(s) that their group came up with.

Problem-solving Model

For practical day-to-day problems you can help students to think through the questions or difficulties or issues by encouraging them to use a problem-solving model, see Figure 4.1. By using such a model, students are encouraged to reflect and analyse the problem and then to consider objectively a range of options or alternative solutions. Judgments and decisions made in haste can be regretted as a more appropriate or creative solution might be missed.

A Problem Solving Approach

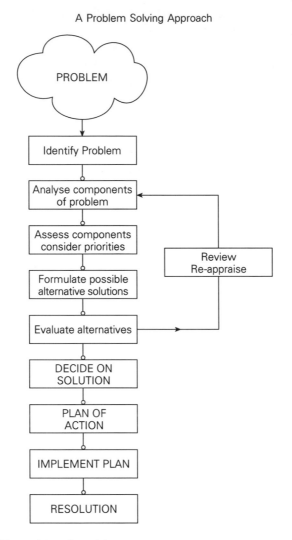

Figure 4.1   Problem-solving: A model

Chapter 4   Proformas

4.1   Developing Time Management Skills
4.2   Daily Task List
4.3   Weekly Daily Planner-Friday
4.4   Weekly Daily Planner-Saturday
4.5   Weekly Daily Planner-Sunday
4.6   Weekly Daily Planner-Monday
4.7   Reflection
4.8   Time Management Monthly Planner
4.9   Balancing Lifestyles
4.10 Developing Listening Skills
4.11 Developing Presentation Skills
4.12 Peer Evaluation: Presentation Skills Including:
        Teaching and Learning Development Plan

Developing Time Management Skills   Proforma 4.1

In the list that follows there are 24 events and tasks to be fitted into four days. Using your usual method of organizing your time decide which of these tasks/events you wish to accomplish/deal with in the time allowed. Use the timetable sheet to plan when you will perform or attend each task/event.

You have 30 minutes for this task.

Events and Tasks

You have had bad toothache on and off since yesterday morning.

Saturday is a relative's birthday. You have not bought a card or present.

You have not phoned, written or visited home since Christmas.

There is the chance of a job a couple of evenings a week, but you would have to go and see someone about it either this evening or tomorrow evening.

There is a *Horizon* programme on TV tomorrow evening at 8pm which your tutors feel is very relevant to the work you are doing at present.

Tonight's TV schedule includes as usual *Neighbours, Home and Away* and *Coronation Street*. Tomorrow is much the same, but there is also *Top of the Pops* and *EastEnders*.

You have a book out of the library which is due back tomorrow.

You have been invited to a friend's in London this weekend. You will need to pack and make travel arrangements.

You need to photocopy an assignment before you hand it in on Friday.

You have a lab session from 2.00–4.00 tomorrow.

You owe someone £10 and they will be in your 2.00–4.00 lab tomorrow.

Remember you have to travel to and from university.

You have a lecture and seminar tomorrow from 9.00–11.00.

Your personal tutor has put up a note asking to see you as soon as possible.

You have no clean underwear left!

It would be advisable to eat and shower at some time.

You have been assigned a group project — the group has arranged to meet at 6pm tomorrow for one hour.

You need to get some money from somewhere — you only have 89p on you.

Everyone is going out for a drink tonight.

You missed a lecture last week — it might be advisable to copy up the notes before the class on Monday.

You did not finish all the work in the lab session yesterday — it needs to be done before next week.

Proforma 4.1 (cont'd)

A friend wrote to you four weeks ago — it is your turn to write or phone. A major assignment is due in at 9am on Monday morning. You have not yet done the library research, the writing and the word-processing. This will take up to 15 hours of work, and you will lose 5 per cent of your mark each day it is late.

You have invited your lover round for a candle lit dinner tomorrow evening. There is no food (or anything else) in the house!

You have a mid-sessional exam in three weeks' time.

Reflection

Whether we are aware of it or not, we make decisions about how to use our time on the basis of our values and goals.

Goals are our ambitions and desires — what we want to achieve. Goals should spring directly from our values. If not, we are unlikely to attain that particular goal, since we shall be working against ourselves.

Goals cannot usually be achieved by a single action alone, but usually take time and many activities before they are realized.

Maintenance tasks are those that are essential to our everyday functioning, like washing, eating, sleeping. Progress tasks are those that get us nearer to our goals, such as studying, completing assignments, and so on. Urgent tasks are those that need to be done in the next few hours or so, important tasks are those that need to be done at some time, but not necessarily immediately. Coping with urgent, maintenance tasks can often mean that the important progress tasks do not get done.

In planning our time, we make conscious or unconscious decisions based upon our values and goals. The ways in which each of you chose to spend the weekend in this simulation was based upon these inmost feelings about what is important. It can be very helpful to be clear about our priorities and to make sure that we address these in disposing of our time. It can also be essential to plan ahead to make sure that priority items do not become impossible to cover.

| **Daily Task List** | | Proforma 4.2 | |

LIST the small tasks to be done during the day.
In the status box indicate the stage of completion periodically, for example

* *   *in progress (for tasks that may take a day or two)*
* ✔   *tasks completed*
* →   *tasks planned forward to another day* (specify day/date if possible)

TASK DETAILS	STATUS	TASKS DETAILS	STATUS

	DATE	TIME	DETAIL	• **COMMENTS** • **SUB-TASKS** • **ASSOCIATED TASKS**
			Weekly/Daily Planner **— Friday** Proforma 4.3	
F R I D A Y		0600		
		0700		
		0800		
		0900		
		1000		
		1100		
		1200		
		1300		
		1400		
		1500		
		1600		
		1700		
		1800		
		Evening		

© Falmer Press

	DATE	TIME	DETAIL	• COMMENTS • SUB-TASKS • ASSOCIATED TASKS
			Weekly/Daily Planning — Saturday	Proforma 4.4
S A T U R D A Y		0600		
		0700		
		0800		
		0900		
		1000		
		1100		
		1200		
		1300		
		1400		
		1500		
		1600		
		1700		
		1800		
		Evening		

	DATE	TIME	DETAIL	• **COMMENTS** • **SUB-TASKS** • **ASSOCIATED TASKS**
			Weekly/Daily Planner **— Sunday** Proforma 4.5	
S U N D A Y		*0600*		
		0700		
		0800		
		0900		
		1000		
		1100		
		1200		
		1300		
		1400		
		1500		
		1600		
		1700		
		1800		
		Evening		

© Falmer Press

	DATE	TIME	DETAIL	• COMMENTS • SUB-TASKS • ASSOCIATED TASKS
			Weekly/Daily Planner **— Monday** Proforma 4.6	
M O N D A Y		0600		
		0700		
		0800		
		0900		
		1000		
		1100		
		1200		
		1300		
		1400		
		1500		
		1600		
		1700		
		1800		
		Evening		

© Falmer Press

Reflection	Proforma 4.7

Reflect on the process of decision-making, and the process of deciding priorities.

The following questions might help you to think about these matters:

What did you decide to do?

What did you decide not to do?

What does this tell you about your goals?

What does this tell you about your priorities?

To what extent are you influenced by external factors?

Now make a second plan for yourself, thinking about what you have learned from this exercise.
PS Think about the use of a diary or organizer.

Time Management Monthly Planner   Proforma 4.8

MONTH	DATE	DETAILS OF ACTIVITY	COMMENTS ASSOCIATED TASKS
JANUARY			
FEBRUARY			
MARCH			
APRIL			
MAY			
JUNE			

			Proforma 4.8 (cont'd)
MONTH	**DATE**	**DETAILS OF ACTIVITY**	**COMMENTS ASSOCIATED TASKS**
JULY			
AUGUST			
SEPTEMBER			
OCTOBER			
NOVEMBER			
DECEMBER			

Balancing Lifestyle   Proforma 4.9

Do you have the right balance between the time you give to work, recreation, and other activities?
Would you like to spend more time on activities that keep you fit and healthy?
Do you spend as much time as you would like with family and friends?

Complete the following chart.
At present I rate the quality of my life as follows:

	Poor	Adequate	Good	Excellent
Work				
Sleep (amount and quality)				
Social Life				
Leisure and Hobbies				
Health and Exercise				
Self Development — acquisition of personal or professional skills and qualifications				

Developing Listening Skills   Proforma 4.10

We are going to examine the component parts of the process of listening and how we can be more aware of potential difficulties.

Let us consider listening. It is part of the two way communication process which requires the individual to:

- attend to the speaker;
- actively listen to the content of linguistic aspects of communication — speech;
- be aware of the paralinguistics — the timing, tone, accent and volume of speech.

We also need to note that non-verbal behaviour or body language can be indicators of the individual's feelings associated with the context of the spoken word or the context in which the communication has arisen or is arising. We need to be aware of this component of communication from our own perspective and ask the question, What am I going to convey to others?

What strategies can we implement to minimize stress and avoid conveying inaccurate messages?

Attending
We need to develop skills in focusing in on the communication partner; by setting aside our preoccupations during the communication. This 'baggage' interferes with the clarity of our thoughts about the communication itself. It can block our responses within the process and distract us from the necessary observations.

Active observation
In addition we need to practise active observation. The process of communication requires us to notice several aspects of the communication partner as detailed above. You can practise active observation outside the communication process, to develop your skills.

Listening
In this part of the process we need to engage in active listening strategies. Merely catching a message is not sufficient. We need to process the content of the message and 'hear' what and how it is being said. To hear and be fully aware of the message conveyed is to note the content of what is being said, the way it is being said and the feelings behind the communication itself.

Proforma 4.10 (cont'd)

Reflecting

Reflecting on critical communications in terms of what we engage in and retain is a helpful way forward in developing listening skills. Begin to use checking out techniques as ways of ensuring that you have grasped the key issues/components of the communication.

- Ask your partner within the communication to repeat/summarize key points.
- Reflect back your understanding as a form of summarizing.
- Ask for clarification.
- Ask for time to think through the essence of the conversation if you are being asked to make a decision/action which you are not comfortable with.

In releasing the 'baggage' we hold for the period of the communication we are enabling ourselves to 'focus in' and engage in the process. In listening we also need to resist the temptation to think ahead to the next question and or rehearse the next sequence, as this inhibits our full engagement.

If the communication is a planned event then a rehearsal phase can be preparation for the dialogue. You can think through and check out key questions and/or areas which must be included. This is particularly helpful if the planned communication is likely to be difficult in some way.

Listening and hearing in a busy environment is an art, and as such is one which we must all practise. Much can be gained from reflecting upon one's approach to the activity and setting a goal to develop the skills; for effective listening skills can save time, place you under less pressure and boost your confidence when you 'hear' the positives in the conveyance of a message. Passive listening means you miss out: active listening means you stay informed and in tune.

© Falmer Press

Developing Presentation Skills   Proforma 4.11

This exercise is practice to allow you to develop some of the necessary skills prior to your formal assessed presentations.

Form groups of four of five:

- Introduce yourselves to your neighbours group members.
- Generate a list of factors that you think are important in planning and delivering good presentations.
- Put them into an agreed order of priority, listing the most important first and so on.

Preparing a presentation
Prepare a five minute presentation on the factors which your group think are important in planning and delivering an excellent presentation.

Delivering a presentation
Each group in turn will make a five minute presentation on their own factors for excellent presentations. Each member of the group should make a more or less equal spoken contribution to the presentation. The other groups should assess each group on the basis of their own criteria. Each group will be asked to give feedback to each presentation, on the basis of their own criteria.

Debriefing
Your tutor will lead a discussion on the activity as a whole when each group has made its presentation. Your tutor might hand out the criteria for assessment that will be used in the class work assessment or a student self/peer evaluation proforma. To follow up this session your tutor may ask you to complete a teaching development plan. This will assist you in a practical way in developing your teaching style and performance.

Peer Evaluation: Presentation Skills   Proforma 4.12

Presenter's Name/s	KEY	5 Agree
		4 Tend to agree
		3 No opinion
		2 Tend to disagree
		1 Disagree

AREAS TO BE CONSIDERED	5	4	3	2	1
1 ENVIRONMENT					
The room was:					
i) arranged appropriately for the style of session					
ii) arranged to enable the group to see the presenter					
iii) arranged to enable the group to see the AVA					
2 INTRODUCTION					
The introduction was effective in:					
i) arousing interest					
ii) stating the objectives of the session					
iii) setting the 'scene' for the session					
3 THE INDIVIDUAL GROUP MEMBER					
As a member I:					
i) settled into the session					
ii) was interested					
iii) understood the topic/subject presented					
iv) enjoyed the style of the session					
4 THE PRESENTER AND THE GROUP					
The presenter:					
i) maintained contact with the group					
ii) maintained appropriate eye contact					
iii) provided a structure to the session					
iv) responded to the group's needs					
v) maintained the group's interest					
vi) facilitated a comfortable 'climate'					
5 THE DELIVERY					
The presentation material was:					
i) organized					
ii) logical in its sequence					
iii) well paced					
iv) clearly presented					

Presenter's Names/s	KEY	5	Agree
		4	Tend to agree
		3	No opinion
		2	Tend to disagree
		1	Disagree

	5	4	3	2	1
6 THE PRESENTER					
i) spoke clearly					
ii) used appropriate language					
iii) spoke at an appropriate speed					
iv) allowed time for the assimilation of information					
v) allowed time for consolidation					
vi) summarized and concluded effectively					
vii) kept to time					
viii) used appropriate group management techniques					
ix) had no distracting mannerisms					
7 THE CONTENT					
In planning and delivering the material the presenter:					
i) chose appropriate material					
ii) taught the correct level					
iii) met the objectives and the level expected					
iv) met the learners' expectations					
v) used the most appropriate teaching method					
vi) used appropriate audio visual aids					
vii) chose appropriate support material					
8 AUDIO VISUAL AIDS					
In the use of audio visual aids the presenter					
i) used them appropriately to support the content					
ii) was competent in the use of the equipment					
iii) achieved the right balance in the material displayed by this means					

SUMMARY

THE BEST FEATURES OF THE PRESENTATION

FEATURES WHICH REQUIRE DEVELOPMENT

Detailed comments overleaf

**Teaching and Learning
Development Plan** Proforma 4.12 (cont'd)

- Identified areas for development

- Strategies and timescales for implementing practical activities

Signed .... Print Name ....

Teaching Techniques that can Reduce the Pressures on Tutors and Students

This chapter focuses specifically on teaching and assessment techniques that ease pressures. Whilst the main benefits are for tutors, there are positive aspects that have consequences for students by reducing pressures within assignments and easing feelings of anxiety that surround them. In addition, the chapter deals with some issues relating to group dynamics and climate that affect students. As stated earlier, the milieu for learning has a crucial impact on the quality of that learning experience and on students' progress.

Alternatives in Assessment

Marking students' work is an important part of any tutor's responsibilities. Students need the feedback on their progress that having their work assessed can give them. Assessment has tended to become particularly burdensome and stressful in higher and further education as student numbers have increased in recent years. When teaching duties are allocated there is recognition that assessment is an important part of the job, although there is often no allowance given for the fact that bigger modules or courses and greater student numbers can more than double the effort required. A stack of projects or essays can sometimes require as much as one week of working time to assess.

Managing the Assessment Load

To avoid overload, there are several possible ways forward:

- *Review the way you set and mark assignments.*
  Use group assignments. This can be very effective since it can cut the marking load by around 75 per cent, compared with setting individual pieces of coursework. At first sight this strategy has great potential, but you need to consider the following:

— Students need support in learning to work effectively as members of a group or team (see **Building Teams** in Chapter 2, p. 8).
— Exceptional students run the risk of being deprived of the true recognition of their contribution if the level of work and performance of the other group members is of a lesser standard.
— The range of marks may be compressed or enhanced unexpectedly, depending upon the task and the skills that students are asked to display.
— The greatest clarity is needed in launching the group or team work, in specifying the criteria for success, and operational procedures, such as the frequency and regularity of team meetings and the taking of minutes, for instance.

- *Review the objectives for the particular unit of study and then match these with alternative forms of assessment.*

  For example:

Type of aims and objectives	*Appropriate assessment*
Low level (recall, describe, list etc.)	Short answer and objective tests
Medium level (compare, contrast)	Oral presentations
Higher level (critically analyse, evaluate, synthesize)	Essay, project

- *Review your own preferences in the context of the module objectives.*
  Ask *'Where do I get the greatest pleasure or satisfaction in my role as assessor? Do I enjoy assessing essays or presentations, for example?'*
  There is obviously an important place for the traditional essay, seminar presentations and examinations, but it is possible to introduce alternatives into these that preserve the form but reduce the assessment load.

- *Consider the range and scope of assignments.*
  Consider with a view to:
  — reducing the word limit;
  — redefining the depth of knowledge that you wish to examine;

— altering the style of the assignment so that for instance you ask for an outline plan, or a report instead of an essay, or for an abstract or a summary statement.

- *Try to meet students' needs.*
  Ask for more frequent, but much shorter, coursework assignments so that you can alleviate some pressures on students and give them more frequent feedback.

- *Establish schedules of coursework.*
  Coordinate launch and submission dates on a module and, if possible, on a course-wide basis. This requires negotiation with colleagues. If an even distribution of course-work is achieved, pressure points are reduced or avoided for students. Well run subject groups or course teams do this smoothing of the assessment load as a matter of routine. This can be taken to the point where each member of the team negotiates annual assessment load with their manager, thus avoiding overload. This approach also makes it easier to meet Examination Board deadlines.

Setting Group Assignments

It is not uncommon for tutors to set group assignments in the expectation that this will reduce the assessment load for both students and tutors alike. The sharing and potential security of being in a group can for many students reduce the feelings of stress that comes with individual assignments. For tutors, if students work in groups of four then the potential savings of time spent on assessment can theoretically be 75 per cent. However, it is crucial to set the scene and prepare the students carefully for the fact that the assessment of group work takes a different form than the marking of individual work. For both it is very important to cover the criteria for success as fully as possible at the launch of the assignment. For group work there must be a well defined set of criteria which will be applied to cover the quality of the product and that of the individual and group contribution to the whole.

A criticism of this approach is that each student only contributes 25 per cent of the content of the assignment and therefore this potentially restricts students' learning. However, the likelihood is that students will encounter ideas which alone they would not have considered and, additionally, they develop skills that enhance their performance in group work.

Setting group assignments allows the tutor to call upon students to display a range of behaviour far greater than they could ask from an individual. For example, groups can be asked to develop posters (with or without a formal presentation), debates, simulations, team-based practical sessions (rehearsal for work-based practice). Innovative ideas can emerge from a brainstorming approach within a group which is not available from individual work.

Group assignments are a positive strategy which can promote enterprise capabilities and, therefore, add a richness to the learning experience. They have the added advantage that, handled properly, they can reduce stress for both students and tutors.

For many more excellent ideas for alternative approaches to assessment see Gibbs, Habeshaw and Habeshaw (1986).

Using Objective Tests

One major contributory factor to work-related pressures and stress is the increased assessment load that accompanies the larger classes now common in tertiary education. This workload can become almost impossible if it involves marking repeated batches of large numbers of essays or reports.

It can be more manageable and, in some cases, academically more appropriate to substitute objective tests for one or more of the traditional written forms of assessment. It can even be a justifiable component of examinations (as in certain GCSE examinations). Objective test items can take many forms, from the true/false, to multiple choice items and beyond. They can be invaluable either in the feedback process when used by students for self-assessment or for more formal assessment.

In going down this road, it is important to be sure that there is an academic 'fit' between the objectives for the module or unit of study and the proposed objective tests. In certain cases, it may be necessary to ratify the proposed change to this form of assessment before a validation panel or similar body. Despite the feeling in some academic circles that objective testing is not a valid approach, there is a lot of evidence that it can perform a useful function. The Open University, for instance, makes extensive use of such tests. It is also a myth that objective test items can only assess such low level objectives as 'state . . .'; 'list . . .' and so on. With care in framing they can also test students' abilities to discriminate, select and analyse. For instance the 'matching pairs' type of question can tax students' abilities quite severely.

Objective tests have other advantages than giving the tutor the ability to assess the results quickly and easily. They also allow frequent feedback to students on their progress and they allow the tutor to assess students across the whole range of the syllabus instead of merely on one or a few topics.

However, there are some actual or potential disadvantages. One is that it can be very time consuming to produce reliable and valid test items. They do need to be framed with care and pilot tested to make sure that they are testing what they are intended to test. However, it might be possible (and much quicker and easier) to use published test items, especially if you can identify a text or other publication that includes a selection of them. Very often, texts originating in the USA incorporate these as a matter of course, either in the text itself or in the accompanying tutor guide. Some US publishers even supply the test items in an appropriate form for use on a computer.

Once you have developed or discovered a batch of test items, it is important to make sure that they are not released to students. When the tests are administered; it will be helpful to collect the questions in at the end of the test. Otherwise, they will be in circulation and next time you use them the odds are that some students will have seen them already.

For further ideas about using objective tests see Gibbs (1985).

Introducing Peer Assessment

Students' time is a relatively untapped resource. Involving them in assessing the work of their peers can relieve tutors of some of the time pressure involved in assessment. It can also be educationally sound, not only because one of the capability or transferable skills that employers look for in recruitment is a person's ability to appraise their own skills and abilities and those of others, but also because marking the work of another challenges students to use their higher intellectual skills of analysis and evaluation. This can also have a demystifying effect because it reveals to students the methods and procedures of assessment that can cause anxiety if they are hidden from them.

If you decide to go down this path, it is best done gradually, using it as a learning process in the early stages and as a recognized means of assessment in the final year where outcomes count.

An obvious requirement for peer assessment to be effective is that the students are very clear about the criteria upon which they will be expected to base their judgments. For instance, it can be excellent training in essay writing for students to start by assessing the work of past students in the form of two essays selected for their differences in approach and academic worth. Some tutors reserve the ultimate right to adjudicate in the formulation of the final mark.

How to run a starter activity: Peer Assessment

Give the students the essays and say:
I want you to assess these essays. Please read them carefully, putting helpful and critical comments in the margin and giving each essay a mark out of 100 at the end.

When they have finished, put the students into pairs and say:
In your pairs, you have five minutes to compare your comments and the marks you gave to each essay. Discuss the reasons for any similarities and differences.

Then put the students into groups of four, five or six and ask them to compare the comments and marks that they gave. Then say:
Now appoint a scribe to take notes and a reporter who will summarize your views at the end. In the next 20 minutes I want each group to make a list of the criteria for excellent essays, and to put the list into priority order.

After 20 minutes call on the reporter from each group in turn to call out the next item on that group's list of criteria. Write each point on the board, ohp, flip chart and then discuss any differences in view to arrive at a consensus.
You will end up with the criteria for excellence.

Next ask the students to apply these criteria to the work of their peers. They will probably need to practise before they become confident, and you will want to sample their assessment to ensure some evenness of quality.

You can use the same technique to raise students' awareness of the criteria for excellence in oral presentation (using a video) and in report writing by using sample reports instead of essays.

Particularly in the final year of a course students can become very competent at this and they can be immensely helpful to one another in giving feedback orally that would take a tutor many hours in one-to-one tutorials.

Introducing Self Assessment

Students sometimes try to manoeuvre tutors into a position where they are the sole provider of information and the lone assessor of their work. This is a potential stress factor, because under these conditions the tutor is tempted to take all the responsibility for the students' progress. Tutors in this situation tend to increase the pressures on themselves by trying to cover the whole syllabus in class — at the risk of superficiality — and taking the responsibility for giving feedback to students through frequent assessments.

This is contrary to the philosophy and aims of further and higher education which is to develop motivated learners who are well able to judge the quality of their own performance. By the time students graduate, they should have a very good idea of the quality of their work and, in many cases, they should be able to assess it as effectively as their tutor can. The sooner we can cultivate in our students the notion of independence in learning, the more effective and efficient they will become. Being able to assess one's own work is both an important signal of independence for students and a support mechanism for them.

This process can begin in the first year, or even at induction, when you can make students aware of the planned sequence of development that will take place over the three or four years of their course.

Introduce students to the criteria for excellent essays and reports by using self assessment activities.

How to run the activities: Encouraging Self Assessment

Essay or Report Marking

Before the students first write an essay (or report) it is well worth giving them the experience of considering the criteria for excellent essays and reports and the expectations according to the year or level of studies.

Divide the students in groups of four, and ask them to share their ideas and then to appoint a scribe and a reporter and to make a list (on acetate or flip chart paper) of what they think are the main criteria for excellent essays.

Collect the main ideas from each group, either by a report back session if the number of groups in your class is quite small, or by collecting an idea in turn from each group if there are a lot of students. Put these ideas on a single sheet for students to use when writing their essay or report.

An alternative activity is as follows:

Devise an essay cover sheet with spaces under each category or criterion. Then ask the students to fill the sheet in before they hand in their essays.

Or alternatively:

Introduce students to the process of reflection (see **Developing Reflective Students**, in Chapter 4, p. 13) and arrange for them to practise this skill in relation to their writing, either before or after they have had feedback on it from you or from their peers.

For further information and ideas about introducing self assessment see Boud (1985).

Maintaining Satisfaction in Teaching

As student numbers increase and as the amount of time we can spend with them collectively and individually decreases, tutors can find themselves being forced into teaching patterns that no longer give them the satisfaction that they used to enjoy. In these circumstances, it is easy to become demotivated and disillusioned. If this seems to be happening to you, it might be worth asking: *What aspects of my teaching give (or gave) me most satisfaction?* and once you have identified what these are then ask yourself: *What can I do to reorganize my teaching to restore some of the enjoyment?* For instance, you might get most pleasure in seeing the students in small groups. It might be a long haul and hard work, but it might be possible, using resource-based learning or some similar technique (see earlier in this chapter), to reorganize your teaching time so that you can run 'surgery sessions' either by appointment or on an *ad hoc* basis for at least some of your teaching time.

Being Creative about Your Teaching Time

As universities and colleges suffer further cuts in the unit of resource, they are being forced to make further so-called 'efficiency gains'. The tendency under such circumstances is to put teaching staff under pressure to 'teach' as many students at a time as possible — hence there is a move towards bigger and bigger groups of students in lectures and seminars. This is fine if you enjoy lecturing to ever larger groups, or if you believe that students learn much in lectures.

For most tutors, their role is about providing the appropriate circumstances in which students can learn effectively, and this does not include addressing hundreds of students in lectures. Under the pressure of increasing student numbers, you need to be creative about using the ever-more precious teaching time that you are allocated. You also need to be selfish, to arrange your teaching to suit your own preferences and enthusiasms in order to restore or maintain some job satisfaction. If you don't do this, no-one will do it for you. One approach is to consider what is the most important aspect of your face to face teaching role, and to concentrate on providing this whilst using other techniques for supplying the rest of the teaching support. For instance, you might decide that the provision of academic support through seminars is the most important teaching task because it does more than anything else to enable students to reach their learning objectives for your course or module. This might mean that you decide to invest all your contact time in inducting the students into a new learning environment and in leading or acting as guide and mentor to students learning in groups.

The exact techniques that you employ to achieve all this will be up to your creativity, but the sort of options that you might consider are:

- supplemental instruction or something similar by which students provide support for one another (Wallace, 1996);
- a course text — perhaps with a commercial study guide or a 'wrap around' guide that you create yourself;
- the opportunity for students to gain continuous feedback from some automated system such as 'Questionmark';
- tutorial support via E–mail to yourself or to a well briefed and trained research assistant.

The exact combination of elements that you eventually come up with will depend upon your own circumstances and the needs of your students.

Your creativity is needed to plan and operate the course or module. Here are some practical ideas for supporting students whilst using your teaching time creatively. See that they:

- have easy access to the information they need, such as a time-table or schedule for the course or module;
- receive sufficient and appropriate feedback;

- feel a sense of belonging;
- undertake sufficient assignments at the appropriate level, perhaps through a learning agreement;
- feel supported in their work.

It will probably repay you to evaluate carefully the progress of your students under the new regime that you have designed and their perceptions of its effectiveness for them. It can be very useful to have a formative evaluation after a few weeks so that you can reassure yourself that things are going well, or that you need to institute any changes necessary to further improve and refine the operation of the module or course. This interim and final evaluation can be very helpful as the basis for conference papers or publications about your new approach and its effectiveness.

Balancing Strategies for Control and Independence

If we increase the amount of independent learning that our students do, then this can help to ease our workload. It can also increase or at least maintain our effectiveness as tutors: especially if the strategies for independent learning are well thought out and properly supported. It will also help to achieve the philosophical aims of further and higher education: to educate self-motivated and self-aware learners.

The concepts of control and independence can be very productive frames through which to view the job of teaching, not least because looking at the task in this way can highlight areas of work that are taking time unnecessarily, or that are becoming increasingly burdensome and stressful.

Control strategies are those that we use to ensure that the students, for whom we are responsible, are learning. They include such devices as assignments with deadlines, required reading, tests and so on. For many of us, not only do they enable us to keep a record of students' progress, they also reassure us that some learning is happening. This can be very important, and all courses need some control strategies.

By contrast, independence strategies allow the students a greater degree of freedom in what and how they learn. Using student-led seminars, problem-based learning, learning agreements and group work, in which students have the latitude to set their own agenda, can be very effective in allowing students to take more responsibility for their own learning.

One way of sustaining students as they work independently is to encourage or schedule their use of an interim check list or a review of their objectives, just to make sure that they are still on course.

Using a judicious mix of control or independence strategies is partly what makes modules and units of study different from one another and stimulating for students. Managing any combination of either is hard work, but reappraising the mix and inducting students carefully into the roles expected of them can be a stimulus and a challenge for them and the tutor.

Giving General Feedback to Students

Students frequently report that they have insufficient feedback on their progress through the year. Lack of such feedback lowers the self-esteem of many students, lowers their confidence and increases their uncertainty and anxiety possibly to the point where their academic performance is adversely affected.

Experience suggests that students think that feedback has to come from tutors and has to relate to formal coursework assignments and grades. However, feedback of this nature is only one type in a range from which students can benefit. It is, therefore, important to be explicit at the beginning of the module or course about the types of feedback that will be used, and when it will occur. The timing can be laid out in the module timetable or schedule.

The following types of feedback can each help students in their learning:

- written reviews of coursework assignments;
- examination grades;
- peer group comments/formal evaluation following student-led seminars/presentations;
- tutor evaluations of student-led seminars/presentations:
    verbal feedback following a session;
    written evaluation using forms with criteria listed;
- self assessment linked to student activities;
- video playbacks — these are useful in group work, experiential learning, student-led seminars and presentations and can take the form of:
    tutor's commentary on the video;
    students' self assessment on the video;
    tutor and student partnership in assessing the video and discussing the outcomes;

- laboratory or work-based learning supervision;
- computer aided learning packages.

Setting Ground Rules for and Giving Feedback on Assignments

Assignments are a fundamental part of teaching and learning. Handled carelessly or inappropriately, they can produce anxiety in students and stress in tutors. Students do need feedback on their course work assignments in addition to grades/marks to assist them in their learning and prepare them for future work, which inevitably becomes more complex.

How to run the activity: Coursework Briefing

Preparation before you launch the assignment (see Proforma 5.1 on p. 95).

Prepare an assignment briefing sheet which includes the following guidelines for the students:

the launch date and submission date;

arrangements for the submission e.g. collected in session x or signed in at the school office;

assignment details i.e. the questions/the task;

specifics or a range of references which may be of help in completing the work set;

statement regarding the reference system to be used;

statement on plagiarism;

the name and room number of the module leader in case of academic queries.

How to launch the assignment

Be explicit to the student group verbally. Arrange a time to discuss the guidelines (this may be following a timetabled lecture or another mutually convenient time). Confirm the meeting arrangements on a poster for the notice board. (It is essential that all students have the potential opportunity to attend and, therefore, not be disadvantaged in any way.) Once the arrangements have been made, abide by them. It is all too easy to be forced into conducting one to one briefing sessions and this can become too demanding. Some students also feel that recipients of these sessions have somehow received an unfair advantage.

Providing feedback after the assignment is completed (see Proforma 5.2 on p. 96).

Provide individual feedback on the assignment itself. This can be carried out in various ways that can reduce the demands that students make upon tutors outside formal hours and therefore reduce stress levels. For instance:

> Use a review sheet of written comments that focuses specifically on the following:
>> presentation
>> content
>> the use of resources
>> the degree of integration between theoretical concepts and practical application
>> areas and strategies for future development
>
> Give general feedback to the class as a whole. This can highlight the principles and approaches which might have been taken and can be a forum in which to address general queries. This helps to place a perspective on the assignment overall and guidelines on which to draw for future submissions. In addition, it should reduce the number of queries for which students knock on the office door for 'just a minute' and are still in the room ten minutes later!
>
> Provide a one-to-one tutorial and guidelines for students who have failed assignments. (This should be from the tutor who marked that student's work.)

Provide a note on the implications of the failure to complement the above.

Use carbonized review sheets — the top sheet for the student for future reference, a second sheet for your records and the third available for the external examiner.

Facilitating Peer Feedback

What others think of us and what we do is a critical component of our development and of our self-esteem and our interpersonal and intra personal skills. Feedback is a means of learning more about ourselves, the way we interact and the effect that our actions have on other people. Peer feedback was mentioned in the preceding section as a helpful means of giving general feedback to students. If feedback is to be meaningful and acceptable to an individual, then it must be offered genuinely and in a constructive way. Giving feedback is, therefore, a skill and one that must be developed in student groups if peer feedback is to be a helpful and positive feature.

In developing these skills it will be helpful to make sure that the students are fully aware of any criteria on which they are providing peer feedback. Otherwise, they can make wrong assumptions that increase rather than reduce stress and uncertainty — which is the purpose of the activity.

Techniques that students should use in giving peer feedback:

- Provide encouragement and highlight the strengths;
- If necessary, identify the weaknesses or aspects for development (it is more likely that these will be heard and acted upon if they are presented in a positive way);
- Avoid generalizations. General comments do not enable an individual to learn as there is insufficient information from which to build a new strategy. It is more helpful to build a new strategy if this is discussed in terms of specific detail and precise examples;
- Refer to behaviour that can be changed;
- Provide a positive that will assist a negative — for example, in detailing weaknesses or areas for development offer a positive alternative that can be used (it may not be accepted, of course, but it can help and individual to understand the type of alternative strategy they need to consider);
- Avoid good or bad. Be descriptive; it tells the recipient what you experienced. There are no dimensions to good or bad;
- Accept ownership. It is the giver's experiences that are being offered in the process of feedback. Therefore, it should be expressed as 'I felt that' rather than statements of global fact;
- Allow choice. Remember that it is the recipient's decision whether or not to accept the feedback offered, or act upon it. When they are giving feedback to one another, students should be honest and genuine and avoid being prescriptive but offer options. It is much more likely that the recipient will respond to this type of approach. Being prescriptive can increase anxiety, cause resentment and might hinder the process of learning.

In the initial stages of such an activity students will require support, reassurance and guidance until they feel confident in their abilities to provide peer feedback. Once established it can be a valuable means of support for the learning process both in academic terms and for personal growth.

Handling Difficult Groups

From time to time, all groups go through a difficult phase. Normally, this occurs at high pressure times. For example, just prior to the examination period, on return from work-based learning placements. The classroom environment is dynamic in nature and the 'baggage' that students bring with them is influential to the way that a session progresses.

How do you resolve the difficulties?

A sound principle is to develop your awareness of what is actually going on in terms of the group dynamics. Increasing your knowledge about the way the group operates will help you to spot potential difficulties and address them.

If a group is struggling with issues for too long a great sense of disenchantment can arise, which causes feelings of tension and stress. It is therefore worth you devoting some time during and immediately following the session to reflect upon the following:

- the nature of the activity;
- the performance of the group;
- the processes within the group; how the group is working.

From this form of active observation and reflection you can identify some of the crucial elements which influence the dynamics. For example:

- the group's level of participation;
- individuals who influence the group;
- individuals who withdraw from the group;
- levels of socio-emotional activity; listening, attending, supporting, helping;
- the emergence of roles within the group; are there leaders, for example?

From this point it is possible to introduce changes in the way the group operates to eliminate the problems.

Chapter 5   Proformas

5.1   Coursework Briefing
5.2   Coursework Feedback

Coursework Briefing	Proforma 5.1

Module title   **Module code**

Launch date   **Submission date**

Submission Procedures
Detail where students hand in work, any signing in procedures and the deadline time. You may indicate that the work will be accepted the week in which the deadline exists to avoid any administrative confusion if several assignments are due within a given period. Alternatively you may collect assignment in at the start of a teaching session

Statement on Plagiarism
Detail a user friendly description of plagiarism and how to avoid it. Refer to or add in a direct quotation of the regulations that your institution uses.

Briefing

- Provide instructions on the assignment e.g. the range of choice one out of three etc.
- Insert the question/s or in the case of a project or group task the framework in which the students will work
- Identify any resources which must be used if this appropriate
- Identify the referencing system to be used

Coursework Criteria
Detail the assessment criteria to be used and where appropriate the percentage mark awarded for different categories e.g. 10% presentation 10% use of resources 15% integration theory to practical example etc.

Guidance on Resources
Detail references which may be helpful in preparing the assignment.

Tutorial advice
Enter who will be available to offer advice on the assignment and when this will be available. This is particularly important where there is a module team or large numbers of students.

Notes on Preparing the Assignment
The following may be relevant given particular styles of assignment

- use of student number and or name on each sheet
- format for front sheet
- type of binding to be used
- the ruling on page layouts, typeface, sections, appendices/tables/figures

Coursework Feedback		Proforma 5.2	
Module title		**Module code**	
Submission status	on time	late	extension
Assignment title			
Presentation			
Content			
The use of resources			
Degree of integration between theoretical concepts and practical application			
Areas for future development • • • Strategies for development • • •			
Tutor's signature		Mark awarded	

Copy to: student, tutor and external examiner
© Falmer Press

Chapter 6

Partnership and Feedback as a Means of Support for Tutors

It is easy to become isolated or to actively withdraw from the mutual support available through contact with colleagues when we are under pressure or feel that we lack the time to make such contact. It is frequently contact of this kind that sustains and supports a group under otherwise intolerable pressure. Too often, there is a tendency to want to conceal from our colleagues the fact that we are under pressure or feeling stressed. We might fear that it looks like a confession of weakness or inefficiency. However, the likelihood is that once we can bring ourselves to share or confide in a trusted colleague or colleagues, then not only do we open up a channel of strong support but we can often find that colleagues are in similar circumstances. This chapter suggests differing ways of working with colleagues in partnership and thus deriving positive support.

Getting Help from Colleagues

The support can take a number of forms. The most important first line support is simply to voice our concerns to a trusted and empathetic listener. This can sometimes be enough to relieve the pressure and allow us to cope again. Colleagues can also offer practical support, such as sharing the work of preparing important documents by proof reading, copy editing or even co-writing. They might agree to share some difficult teaching for a short time or help to prepare for classes that seem overwhelming. They might agree collectively to form a sustained mutual support group or network that looks out for signs of pressure and stress in one another.

You might also consider whether to consult your manager, who after all is a colleague, too. This can be extremely beneficial in some cases, but disastrous in others and it is important to be clear about whether this is the right move in your circumstances. If in doubt, seek advice from one of the support services identified in Chapter 7.

Ways of approaching your colleagues:

- suggest a meeting for coffee or lunch together either at the college refectory or outside;
- find out when colleagues are free and suggest a meeting at a time to suit them;
- find out who goes to the staff lounge for coffee or tea on a regular basis and arrange to go with them, or meet them there.

Getting Positive Feedback from Colleagues about your Teaching

When the lecture room door closes you are on your own! Establishing networks for support is essential in the survival process, particularly in times of stress. From time to time we all need to 'let off steam', to be reassured 'it's not just me' and to know we are heading in the right direction. Equally, its good to tell someone of your successes.

Large institutions compound the feelings of isolation and modular programmes have not assisted in bringing tutors together easily. What do you do?

- establish links with other tutors in your subject discipline;
- be open and willing to share yourself;
- encourage module team meetings (over coffee is always attractive!).

As relationships and networks establish you will, hopefully, find that the support which the various individuals/network groups provide gives you a sense of purpose, acknowledgement and feedback. Remember the old saying, providing you have an established trusting networks, 'a trouble shared is a trouble halved'. Not only that, networks will let you know when things are going well.

Getting Positive Strokes from Students

Lack of recognition from students and colleagues can compound feelings of stress for an individual tutor. We all need to feel valued to preserve our feelings of self worth. However, in many colleges and universities it is rare for a tutor to receive praise and recognition for work well done — sometimes even during the annual appraisal.

What can we do to ensure that we receive positive feedback? One way of finding out how others see us and our work is to ask for it openly. There are various ways in which tutors can elicit this sort of information from students, and it can have the added benefits of being suitable for inclusion in portfolios and pointing the way towards improving professional standards.

Informal feedback
At the end of a course or module, the tutor might say:
I would like some help to try and find out what you think about this part of the course/module and my teaching on it. Please write down on a piece of paper the three things you would most like to say in answer to this question/these questions that I am going to write on the board/show on the overhead projector.

For example either:
The three best things I like about this part of the course/module and how it has been taught are:
or
The part of the module I liked the best was . . .
The aspects of the module that helped me to learn best were . . .

Accentuate the positive
It can also be very rewarding to emphasize the informal positive feedback that you receive to remind you that you are appreciated:

- display any small gifts, letters and cards on your mantelpiece, desk/wall board in your office;
- when students praise your teaching, allow yourself to hear what they say and enjoy it;
- when writing your self appraisal report give full weight to your achievements and include the above as appendices to your report.

Module Feedback

It is always rewarding to receive praise for effort. A few words of thanks or recognition can go a long way to boosting motivation and self-esteem, and they are a good antidote to stress. (You could use the Proforma 6.1 on p. 106 to gather feedback.) Regrettably, many tutors do not receive such acknowledgment for the quality of their work.

This may be because their managers are not fully aware of how well they are doing.

To make sure that this is not the case, it is wise to keep your manager informed about any feedback you collect that reflects favourably on what you do. If you have used a student feedback questionnaire, or something similar, then you have a fairly straightforward task to summarize the data in a form that a busy manager can easily and quickly assimilate.

In the example on p. 101, you will notice that the replies to each question have been tallied in the data section of the report and that students' written comments have been typed out verbatim. All it needs is a brief written statement such as 'Enclosed, for your information, a summary of the results of a survey of students' opinions about my recently completed module/course in . . .'

Faced with a report of this type (brief, easy to assimilate and full of praiseworthy information) it will be a very disinterested manager who does not respond with a note of praise, and even if they don't, you still have the evidence of excellence to present at your appraisal.

Teaching in a Team

For many tutors the move to a modular scheme has produced an increase in workload and a consequent increase in daily pressures and levels of stress. However, the principles of modularization have also given tutors additional opportunities. An important advantage is the potential to develop small, interdisciplinary teams of tutors. Each tutor comes from a different background, has a different perspective and can draw on a range of skills to provide a variety of approaches to areas of expertise for the students. The modular scheme of work is sub-divided for each tutor to input according to their expertise. This strategy of teaching the module as a team can provide a shared responsibility for each tutor, and a greater range of expertise for students to consult.

Tutors are invariably much more comfortable teaching within their area of expertise rather than being required to 'mug up' and deliver the whole module, of which only a portion is within the individuals' area of expertise. Working outside these boundaries can be very stressful.

The team can also share module/course developments; module difficulties can be shared; the volume of assessment/marking can split amongst the team; and they can become potentially more creative in their future schemes of work.

Module Feedback Report

34 students attended the module, and 27 completed feedback questionnaires were received.

Students used the following code to indicate the extent to which they agreed or disagreed with the statements made below:
1. Strongly disagree 2. Disagree 3. Uncertain 4. Agree 5. Agree strongly

number of replies

		1	2	3	4	5
1.	The aims and objectives of the module/course were made clear to me.	–	–	1	5	21
2.	I feel that the teaching on the module/course was of a high standard.	–	2	6	4	15
3.	I feel that the module/course was carefully designed.	–	–	2	5	20
4.	Enough handout material was given.	–	–	7	4	16
5.	The teaching methods used in the module/course encouraged me to take an active part in it.	2	1	9	5	10
6.	I felt supported during my studies on this module/course.	–	3	5	7	12
7.	I received sufficient information on my progress during the module/course.	–	–	7	7	13
8.	The module/course was well organised.	1	3	3	5	15
9.	The assessment was appropriate.	–	1	4	5	17
10.	Overall I feel that this module/course was a worthwhile learning experience.	–	–	–	2	25

Please write down what you thought were the best things about the teaching on this module/course
This course motivated me strongly (seven similar replies)
I enjoyed the seminar sessions (five similar replies)
I wish my other modules had been taught as well (seven similar replies)
Thank you for a worthwhile learning experience (4 similar replies)

What changes would you recommend in the way this module/course, or the tutor operates?
I think the assessment could have been weighted more towards course work (4 similar replies)
I wish that the course works had been spread out more
I had to work harder for this module than for the others (7 similar replies)

Shared Teaching

Shared teaching can be an effective strategy for modules/courses that involve a high degree of integration, facilitation of students and active groupwork, which can be demanding and stressful for a tutor to handle entirely on his or her own.

The module team can teach the class together. From a manager's perspective this might appear resource-heavy. However, this can be overcome simply by looking at the size of the group and deciding where you wish to include shared teaching in the overall scheme of work. Shared teaching is valuable in the following ways:

- it offers support for the tutors involved;
- different perspectives can emerge in discussions and debates with the group;
- the tutors can each have a role to play in enabling students to participate in experiential learning;
- shared opportunity for de-briefing students and tutors involved;
- shared effort in planning and preparation.

For shared teaching to work effectively there has to be commitment from all of the members involved.

Peer Observation of Teaching

We referred earlier in this chapter to the inherent loneliness of teaching. Initiating a programme of peer observation of teaching with one or two trusted colleagues is one way to overcome this. It also has the potential for personal and professional development. It simply involves inviting someone to discuss your class before you give it, and then having them in to watch you teach. This is normally followed by a session where they give you feedback on areas that you agreed beforehand. Then you provide a similar opportunity for your partner.

At a time when tutors are under greater pressure than ever before this might seem like a further unnecessary burden. But the potential benefits are great. To begin with, the opportunity merely to watch others teach and to discuss their approach and your own in detail afterwards can be a rich opportunity for learning. No two people teach alike and no-one is a perfect tutor, so there is always something more to learn about the process. As committed professionals we are all out to improve our performance and peer observation of teaching gives the opportunity for accelerated development of competencies in the classroom.

Not only that, but it can also provide a strong platform of mutual support amongst the participants. Using the system (see below) each participant rapidly becomes aware of the aims, goals and approaches of the others and it becomes easier and easier to discuss the detail of one's teaching because each comes to know the other's methods and philosophy intimately. There is, therefore, less and less need for detailed introductions and preambles before the substantive issues can be introduced. You can use this system with Proformas 6.2, 6.3 and 6.4 on pp. 107–9.

A suggested system for peer observation of teaching.

Carry out the following:

- Arrange with a trusted colleague (or two) to try out this form of mutual support.
- Choose who will observe whom.
- Arrange a mutually convenient time for the observer to listen to the person who is to teach. (See the section on **Developing Listening Skills** in Chapter 4 if you need guidance on how to listen effectively.) The tutor uses this time to explain what the session will be about, what its purpose is, its place in the course or module, and the approach that he or she intends to take to achieve the goals set for the session. He or she can also highlight any particular aspect of the session or how it is taught or handled that they would like feedback about afterwards. This could take about 20 or 30 minutes (see Proforma 6.2).
- The observer then attends the session, and makes notes if necessary on what they see and hear, and especially on those aspects they have been asked to make specific comments about. Depending on the size of the group the tutor might wish to introduce the observer and to explain the reasons for his/her presence (see Proforma 6.3).
- At a mutually convenient time, preferably as soon as possible after the class, the observer and tutor meet for the feedback session. (Again the section on listening skills from Chapter 4 might be useful pre-reading for this session, together with the **Guidelines for Receiving Peer Feedback** at the end of Chapter 2.) At this time the observer does almost all the talking. It is time for the tutor to listen.
- Time for reflection and learning on the part of the tutor is the necessary final step in the sequence. It will help to set aside

some time for thought and probably some writing time to note the key learning points from the exercise and any resolutions for future action, such as further reading or a change in approach (see Proforma 6.4).

- Then the tutor turns observer to provide a similar opportunity for her/his colleague(s) and the cycle is repeated.

It is worth noting that this process is already well established in some universities and colleges. This might be because it is linked to an existing appraisal scheme, or because it has been encouraged by an enthusiastic manager or staff developer. It is also an intrinsic element in the SEDA (Staff and Educational Development Association) process of accreditation for tutors in higher education. Briefly, this scheme specifies the skills, awareness and competencies that a tutor should show to achieve recognition in the form of accreditation. This award is granted on the basis of evidence presented in a portfolio, the contents of which demonstrate excellence in the various aspects of the tutor's role (SEDA, 1996).

Chapter 6   Proformas

| **Module Feedback** | Proforma 6.1 |

Module Title: **Module Code:**

Name (optional)

Using the number codes detailed, please circle the number which represents your feelings/opinion on the extent to which you agreed or disagreed with the statements below.

1. Strongly disagree   2. Disagree   3. Uncertain   4. Agree   5. Agree strongly

1. The aims and objectives of the module/course
   were made clear to me.   1   2   3   4   5
2. I feel that the teaching on the module/course
   was of a high standard.   1   2   3   4   5
3. I feel that the module/course was carefully
   designed.   1   2   3   4   5
4. Sufficient handout material was given.   1   2   3   4   5
5. The teaching methods used in the module/course
   encouraged me to take an active part in it.   1   2   3   4   5
6. I felt supported during my studies on this
   module/course.   1   2   3   4   5
7. I received sufficient information on my progress
   during the module/course.   1   2   3   4   5
8. The module/course was well organized.   1   2   3   4   5
9. The assessment was appropriate.   1   2   3   4   5
10. Overall I feel that this module/course was a
    worthwhile learning experience.   1   2   3   4   5

Please write down what you thought were the best things about the teaching on this module/course

What changes would you recommend in the way this module/course, or the tutor operates?

Thank you for completing the Module Feedback Form

Observation of Teaching Peer Review   Proforma 6.2

BACKGROUND INFORMATION

Module/unit details:

Session number: Date of session:

Total no. sessions in module/unit:

Venue: Time:

SPECIFIC OBJECTIVES FOR THE SESSION

Relationship of Objectives to Overall Aims and Objectives of
Module/Unit

SESSION PLAN
General outline of the teaching and learning methods (specific Session
Plan please use proforma overleaf)

© Falmer Press

Peer Review Sheet	Proforma 6.3

Were the learning objectives achieved?

Was a positive climate established?
(please detail your observations)

Were the teaching and learning methods appropriate to i) the objectives
ii) the session plan iii) the student group?
(please comment)

Did the delivery meet the needs of the students in terms of style, clarity
of presentation and learning/guidance?

Strengths of the session

Agreed development strategy
(detail as appropriate)

SIGNED: DATE:

© Falmer Press

Observation of Teaching Session Plan   Proforma 6.4

Time	Content	Method	Audio/visual/ Supporting materials

PERSONAL EVALUATION — following the session

© Falmer Press

Institutional Support for Tutors

One of the major problems with the pressure of teaching is that uncontrolled it can produce undesirable levels of stress. This work-related stress can build up over time, often without our being aware that it is happening. If the stress levels are high enough for long enough then the body reacts.

The much-used word 'stress' is derived from the Latin word 'stringere' meaning 'drawing tight'. This is not necessarily the negative state that it is commonly understood to be. A certain amount of stress is necessary for effective functioning in everyday life. It is a natural response for our basic safety needs and optimum performance in activities. It arises from the body's fight or flight mechanism that occurs when a threat or challenge is perceived.

Problems can arise when the body fails to return to a normal state after an active period when it has been under stress. An analogy might be to think of an elastic band holding a rolled up newspaper. The elastice band at rest does not hold the newspaper as a cylindrical roll. For it to make a purposeful contribution to holding the newspaper, it must begin to stretch and work under a small amount of tension. If you were to increase the size of the newspaper twofold, the elastic band would become increasingly strained. If allowed to continue in this way for a long period, one of two things might happen: either signficant damage might occur to the paper (it might become creased or more drastically torn) or the band might snap, unable to cope with the continued strain. If the elastic band had been removed once the specific purpose for rolling the paper had been achieved, then the damage would have been averted and the band returned to a resting state.

Given this analogy, the longer the body is placed under stress, the more likely it is that physical and emotional feelings and behavioural reactions will create discomfort. Continuation of such a heightened state can give rise to longer term problems of stress, which might even manifest itself in serious psychological or physical ill-health. Without recognition of what stress means to you, then you will find it difficult to begin to find strategies and coping mechanisms that might be helpful.

Where should you begin? Just take a moment to think about yourself. Ask yourself whether you can recognize the symptoms of stress and write these down. Next, try to identify any situations or times when you become more stressed. Think about your roles and ask are there any connecting patterns of being stressed and under pressure. Use Proformas 7.1, 7.2 and 7.3 on pp. 117–19 to jot down your thoughts.

Achieving a Balance

When we are under pressure, it is often impossible for us to see the wood for the trees. In other words we concentrate on dealing with the current issues and problems without focusing on the wider issues. Answer the questions and complete the following charts. They might help to provide an alternative view of a desirable balance in your life (see Proforma 7.1).

Do you have the right balance between the time you give to work, recreation and other activities?

Use this section to give yourself specific targets, for example:

Would you like to spend more time on activities to keep you physically fit and healthy?

Do you spend as much time as you would like with family and friends?

How do you see yourself spending your time when you retire?

How will you ensure that you are in a position to achieve these goals when the time comes?

It is necessary that we take time out to ask ourselves these questions to ensure that we maintain a healthy balance in the roles, activities and occupations that we engage in. Without such reflection, we cannot begin to compose meaningful strategies and coping mechanisms (see Proformas 7.2 And 7.3).

If you feel that you need to understand the symptoms of stress in order to recognize them more accurately, then there are many books

Place a tick in the appropriate box

	Poor	Adequate	Good	Excellent
Work				
Sleep (Amount & Quality)				
Social Life				
Leisure/ Hobbies				
Health				
Time for Self-development				

on the booksellers' shelves to help you. These discuss the symptoms of stress specifically and offer techniques to manage all aspects of stress: physical, emotional and behavioural reactions. The books can range from a bedtime reading style (Jones, 1997) to more detailed theoretical work, (Cooper, Cooper and Eaker, 1988). The book you are reading now is different from the above as it will take you, or has taken you, through practical ideas specific to your role as a teacher and in your teaching and learning experiences. The ideas hopefully will assist you in managing the pressures of teaching.

Balancing Work Roles

(This section is written as guidance for you, as a tutor. Chapter 2 considers issues on roles for students.)

What do you do in a day?

The tutors' role is multi-dimensional: teacher, tutor, scholar, counsellor, researcher, administrator, manager, team member, leader (of modules, programmes, subjects, for instance), recruiter (of staff and students), colleague and friend.

Being aware of the multi-dimensional nature of the role is the first step to feeling in control or comfortable. No-one in the tutor role is perfect and no-one is expected to be perfect. Our tendency is to strive to fulfil all of the dimensions as completely as possible. A day in the life of any tutor can be so unpredictable that aspects of the role not envisaged at the outset are brought into play in an instant. Thus, we can only go so far in preparing to manage the daily workload. However, working to a schedule of meetings with individuals and classes does give us a certain amount of control.

The interactive nature of our communication with students in our teaching, or with colleagues, is so uncertain that there is always the potential for the unexpected to arise. Take a look back through your diary and you will get a good idea of the wide variety of roles that you fill. But when we are under pressure, we tend only to see the immediate frustrations and tasks that provoke most anxiety.

Coping with the uncertainly in our work
Remember:

- Plan a month ahead. Consciously build in space in your timetable by booking time for yourself in your diary. With luck this will give you time for the important, strategic but non-urgent tasks, and it will also give you space for fire fighting if necessary.
- Plan to work at home from time to time if this is allowed or encouraged by your employer. It gives you time to be forward thinking, reflective and to catch up.
- Understand and use the process and/or procedures for referring students or colleagues to more appropriate contacts.
- Never be afraid to say 'I need time to think about that before I can give an answer'; or even a plain 'No' if it is not a task or activity that is appropriate for you (see also the section on **Developing Assertiveness** towards the end of Chapter 4).
- Consider all aspects of the role and identify those elements that you feel most comfortable with and those that you feel you need some further development for. All institutions have some form of provision for staff development or teacher education.
- Prioritize those aspects of the role that you wish to pursue in terms of your goals, values and career aspirations.
- You have a choice or a certain degree of choice over how you interpret and carry out the dimensions of your role as a tutor.

Role Expectations

However you see your role, remember that others might see it differently, particularly your manager, your students and your colleagues. It is essential to spend time clarifying your role with those around you. This will avoid additional pressure and stress. If you fail to do this, whilst you might be clear in your own mind, others might have expectations of you that you will be unable or unwilling to fulfil.

It is also worth remembering that, for many students, the principles of balancing their work roles (for being a student is work) are similar to those for teachers. This is especially true for those who have to work to make ends meet. You can adapt the above checklist for use with individuals or groups of students.

Having worked through the ideas and questions in this chapter so far, if you are experiencing feelings of being stressed as well as being under pressure, then you might need to seek help beyond your immediate workgroup or department. Here are a few suggestions:

Getting Help from Support Services

Sometimes, when we are under pressure we can feel very isolated. If this pressure becomes too severe it is important to seek help and advice from a support service. Most colleges, or similar institutions, have a range of services that support individuals under stress:

- the Personnel or Human Resources Department will probably have a welfare officer;
- the counselling service, although it may be intended primarily for students, will normally provide immediate help for academic staff who call at reception. The counsellor may then provide contact with appropriate outside agencies;
- the chaplaincy;
- professional union workers;
- occupational health department.

Before you approach the service of your choice, try to write down an account of the symptoms and/or causes of your stress. This can be very helpful, although revealing confidential information about yourself can be difficult at the best of times. However, it is important to document it so that you can convey accurately how you feel when you meet a person from the service you have identified. Information of this kind will help to focus the time you have together.

An initial contact may be all that you need to help you to cope with your stress levels because simply speaking about the problem to someone else can be very therapeutic. If you need further help and advice the person you contact in the first place will know what support is available within your own institution and outside, and they will help you to identify the most appropriate course of action.

Getting Personnel to Run Training Courses

If you or a group of colleagues identify the need for help with coping with the stresses and strains of your jobs, then a natural service to call on is Personnel — sometimes called Human Resources. In an organization of any size, the Personnel or Human Resources Department will have a training function, perhaps supported by a Training Officer and sometimes a Training Manager with in a department or unit. These people are experienced and competent to arrange training courses or workshops on such topics as stress awareness, stress management, time management, assertiveness and so on. A college or university will normally have a full programme of such events. Find out if such a programme offers workshops on these or similar topics. It might be possible to arrange for a bespoke course for yourself and interested colleagues at a time and a location to suit you.

Chapter 7 Proformas

7.1 Achieving a Balance
7.2 Achieving a Balance
7.3 Achieving a Balance

Achieving a Balance   Proforma 7.1

When we are under pressure, it is often impossible for us to see the wood for the trees. In other words we concentrate on dealing with the current issues and problems without focusing on the wider issues. Answer the questions and complete the following charts. They might help to provide an alternative view of a desirable balance in your life.

- Do you have the right balance between the time you give to work, recreation and other activities? Ideally where would you like to make changes?

- Would you like to spend more time on activities to keep you physically fit and healthy? Ideally where would you like to make changes?

- Do you spend as much time as you would like with family and friends? Ideally where would you like to make changes?

- How do you see yourself spending your time when you retire?

- How will you ensure that you are in a position to achieve these goals when the time comes?

Use this section to think about your own goals for the future
© Falmer Press

	Achieving a Balance		Proforma 7.2

Complete the grid below by placing a tick in the box which is most appropriate

	Poor	Adequate	Good	Excellent
Work				
Sleep (Amount and Quality)				
Social Life				
Leisure/ Hobbies				
Health				
Time for Self-development, e.g. training to enhance personal and professional skills				

Achieving a Balance	Proforma 7.3

Use the space below to set your own goals for the future

- Work activities

- Recreational activities

- Social activities

- Activities to keep you physically fit and healthy

- Home based/family activities

The Way Forward: Reflection and Review

As tutors we each have a unique set of responsibilities, values and interests. The following checklists will enable you to review your day-to-day activities in one or more categories on a regular basis, and they set out details of the many tasks which comprise professional academic work to help you to decide where your priorities lie.

Chapter 8   Proformas

8.1   Teaching
8.2   Development of the Curriculum
8.3   Implementing Curriculum Design
8.4   Evaluating and Reviewing the Curriculum
8.5   Administration
8.6   Developing and Updating your Subject Knowledge
8.7   Research
8.8   Other Professional Activities

Teaching	Proforma 8.1

- *Your values*

Reflect on the values you hold with respect to your teaching.
Is this the area which gives you satisfaction?
Why is this?
How do you feel about your students?
How do you feel about your teaching?

- *Goals*

What particular area(s) of your teaching would you like to develop. How soon?
Use the space below to detail your goals.

Development of the Curriculum: Course, Content and Structure   Proforma 8.2

- *Your values*

Reflect on the values you hold with respect to your curriculum development activities.

Is this the area which gives you satisfaction?

Why is this?

How do you feel about your modules/courses?

How do you feel about curriculum development and planning with your colleagues?

- *Goals*

What particular area(s) of curriculum development would you like to develop? How soon?

Use the space below to detail your goals.

Implementing Curriculum Design   Proforma 8.3

Ideas

- Defining teaching and learning strategies.
- Planning and allocating resources.
- Writing schemes of work and lesson plans.
- Preparing assignments and learning materials.
- Developing a variety of modes of learning.
- Identifying the specific needs of students.
- Relating demand for courses to resource implications.
- Assessing the requirements of the wider community.
- Planning a curriculum which is flexible and relevant.

Use the space below to note your ideas and strategies for course design.

**Evaluating and Reviewing
the Curriculum**   Proforma 8.4

Ideas

- Evaluating the curriculum aims in relation to outcomes.
- Appraising teaching methods in the light of student performance.
- Considering student feedback and comments from colleagues.
- Reviewing the evaluation and reporting the findings.
- Suggesting modifications as a result of the review.
- Becoming active in course review and validation — internal and/or external.

Use the space below to identify your personal goals and or course related strategies for the next academic year.

Administration   Proforma 8.5

- *Your values*

Reflect on the values you hold with respect to your administrative activities. How do you feel about your administrative duties?
How do you feel about performing administrative tasks with your colleagues?

- *Goals*
- What practical strategies could you implement to become more efficient and effective?
- What particular abilities would you like to develop? How soon?

This checklist might give you some further ideas about what your goals might be. For instance:

Would you like to be more knowledgeable/active/consistent in:

- keeping student records.
- using data recording and analysing systems.
- developing IT skills.
- planning and organizing courses.
- reviewing and evaluating courses.
- marketing courses (e.g. market research, needs analysis, advertising, design and dissemination of materials, selling).
- interviewing prospective students.
- understanding the decision-making and organizational structure of the college/university.
- participating in the university's committees and other meetings.
- managing and contributing to meetings or working parties.
- arranging courses or departmental timetables.
- budgeting and controlling budgets.
- allocating or bidding for resources.
- organizing and managing laboratories, or studios, or workshops.
- obtaining outside funding for projects and courses.
- liaison with external agencies, employers etc.

Use the space overleaf to identify your personal goals and strategies.

Administrative activities . . .

| **Developing and Updating your Subject Knowledge** | Proforma 8.6 |

• *Your values*

Reflect on the values you hold with respect to your subject knowledge and the process of updating it.

Is this the area which gives you satisfaction?

Why is this?

How do you feel about your subject and its current perspective?

How do you feel about sharing subject knowledge and updating it with your colleagues?

Do you engage in informal professional development?

• *Goals*

What particular area(s) of your subject knowledge and updating would you like to develop? How soon?

This checklist might give you some further ideas about what your goals might be.

- reading current literature.
- developing a database of references and sources.
- subject discussions/seminars with colleagues.
- visiting exhibitions, industry, commerce to observe current methods and trends in your area.
- gathering and structuring information from company employees and others in your subject area.
- observing teaching in your subject in the university and elsewhere.
- discussing appropriate teaching strategies with colleagues in your own and related areas.
- attending conferences, workshops etc. in your subject.
- locating information in your subject area and how it is taught.
- carrying out a project or research.
- doing consultancy work.
- serving on professional/validating/examining bodies.
- identifying changes in your subject area due to modern technology.

Use the space overleaf to identify your strategies for updating in the current and next academic year.

Proforma 8.6 (cont'd)

Developing and updating your subject knowledge . . .

Research	Proforma 8.7

- *Your values*

Reflect on the values you hold with respect to your research.

Is this the area which gives you satisfaction?

Why is this?

How do you feel about research with your colleagues?

- *Goals*

What particular area(s) of your research activities would you like to develop? How soon?

This checklist might give you some further ideas about what your goals might be.

Would you like to be more active/knowledgeable in:

- carrying out personal research in your own discipline or in teaching and learning.
- conducting group research in your own discipline or in teaching and learning.
- supervising or advising on the research work of others.
- selecting appropriate methods for sampling and collecting data.
- designing questionnaires or surveys
- bidding for external funding
- engaging in cross-institution research
- engaging in/developing research networks

Use the space below to identify your ideas and strategies to engage in research activities.

Other Professional Activities   Proforma 8.8

- *Your values*

Reflect on the values you hold with respect to your other professional activities.

How do you feel about your professional activities in the areas you have defined?

- *Goals*

What particular area(s) of your professional activities would you like to develop? How soon?

This checklist might give you some further ideas about what your goals might be. For instance:

Would you like to be more competent/active/consistent in:

- writing textbooks, computer programmes, or learning materials for use inside and/or outside the university?
- writing for in house, local or national press, or professional journals?
- membership of your professional body?
- providing information and advice on careers?
- contributing to local or national radio or TV?
- acting as external examiner, moderator, or assessor for other universities, FE colleges, schools, professional bodies?
- representing the university or your profession in schools, industry, commerce, training organizations?

Use the space below to detail the activities you wish to engage in and how you will achieve this.

AND FINALLY . . .

We hope you have found some of the ideas in this book helpful, and that you can see the benefits of taking positive steps to adapt and develop in a climate of continuous change. The strategies and suggestions that we have made are not the only ways forward and they are proposed, not only to address some of the immediate problems that you face, but also to stimulate your own (and your students') personal and professional development.

We should be delighted if you felt able to write to us to let us know about similar approaches that have worked for you.

We leave the final word to John Ruskin (1851):

> In order that people may be happy in their work, these three things are needed: they must be fit for it; they must not do too much of it; and they must have a sense of success in it.

Bibliography

BOUD, D. (1988) *Developing Student Autonomy in Learning*, 2nd Edn, London: Kogan Page.

BOUD, D. (1995) *Enhancing Learning Through Self Assessment*, London: Kogan Page.

BURGE, L. (1989) 'Beyond andragogy: Some explorations for learning design', *Journal of Distance Education*, Spring.

BURNARD, P. (1992) *Effective Communication Skills for Health Professionals*, London: Chapman Hall.

BURTON, G. and DIMBLEBY, R. (1995) *Between Ourselves*, 2nd Ed, London: Edward Arnold.

CAMPBELL, J. (1990) *Speak for Yourself*, London: BBC Books.

COOPER, C.L., COOPER, R.D. and EAKER, L.H. (1988) *Living with Stress*, Harmondsworth: Penguin.

COX, S. and GIBBS, G. (1994) *Course Design for Resourse Based Learning in the Social Sciences*, Oxford: Oxford Centre for Staff Development.

COX, S. and HEAMES, R. (1997) 'Reducing stress in teaching and learning', in Armstong, S., Thompson, G. and Brown, S. (eds) *Facing up to Radical Changes in Universities and Colleges*, London: Kogan Page.

FISH, D. (1989) *Learning Through Practice in Intitial Teacher Training*, London: Kogan Page.

GIBBS, G. (ed.) (1985) *Alternatives in Assessment 2: Objective Tests and Computer Applications*, Standing Conference on Educational Development, Paper 21, SEDA.

GIBBS, G. (1992) *Improving the Quality of Student Learning*, Oxford: Technical and Educational Services.

GIBBS G., HABESHAW, S. and HABESHAW, T. (1986) *53 Interesting Ways to Assess Your Students*, Oxford: Technical and Educational Services.

HANDY, C. (1990) *The Age of Unreason*, London: Arrow Books.

HOPSON, B. and SCALLY, M. (1981) *Lifeskills Teaching*, Maidenhead: McGraw Hill.

JONES, H. (1997) *I'm Too Busy to be Stressed*, London: Hodder and Stoughton.

KNOWLES, M.S. (1970) *The Modern Practice of Adult Education*, Association Press.

KOLB, D.A. (1984) *Experiential Learning Experience as the Source of Learning Development*, Prentice Hall.

MITCHELL, L. (1987) *Simple Relaxation: The Mitchell Method For Easing Tension*, (2nd Edn), London: John Murray.

PORRITT, L. (1990) *Interaction Strategies*, 2nd Edn, London: Churchill Livingstone.

RAWLINSON, J.G. (1981) *Creative Thinking and Brainstorming*, Farnborough: Gower.

RUSKIN, J. (1851) *Pre-Raphaelitism*, London: Smith Elder and Co.

RUST, C. and WALLACE, J. (1994) *Helping Students to Learn From Each Other*, Paper 86, Birmingham: Staff and Educational Development Association.

SEDA (1996) *Accreditation of Teachers in Higher Education*, Birmingham: Staff and Educational Development Association.

SCHAEF, A.W. (1990) *Meditations for Women Who Do Too Much*, London: Harper Collins.

WALLACE, J. (1996) 'Peer tutoring: A collaborative approach', in Wolfendale, S. and Corbett, J. (eds) *Open Doors: Learning Support in Higher Education*, London: Cassell.

Index